The Kind Mind Method

The Kind Mind Method

One Simple Thought Process
A Universe of Positivity to Explore

ALEXANDER WALTON

Disclaimer:
This book is intended to offer guidance and strategies for cultivating positivity and kindness as a means to reduce negative thinking and enhance your overall well-being. The techniques and concepts presented in this book are based on the author's personal experiences and insights.

Please remember that your mental health journey is a personal one, and there is no one-size-fits-all solution. "The Kind Mind Method" aims to provide you with tools and insights to promote positivity and kindness, but your well-being is of the utmost importance. Prioritise seeking professional help if needed, and use the strategies in this book as part of a holistic approach to self-care and personal growth.

Paperback ISBN: 978-1-7395115-0-0
eBook ISBN: 978-1-7395115-1-7

For Clare

"Be kind whenever possible.
It is always possible."

—DALAI LAMA XIV

"The ideals which have lighted my way, and time after time have given me new courage to face life cheerfully, have been Kindness, Beauty, and Truth."

—ALBERT EINSTEIN

"What counts in life is not the mere fact that we have lived. It is what difference we have made to the lives of others that will determine the significance of the life we lead."

—NELSON MANDELA

"Carry out a random act of kindness, with no expectation of reward, safe in the knowledge that one day someone might do the same for you."

—PRINCESS DIANA

"When words are both true and kind,
they can change the world."

—BUDDHA

CONTENTS

AUTHOR'S NOTE

In December 2015, a number of festive-looking envelopes appeared randomly around cities in the UK. Each one had a message on the front inviting the finder to open it. Within each of the envelopes was a story. An emotional story about a man called Matt who was going through a difficult time. And then, in almost magical circumstances, he received a gift that changed his life. This same gift was inside the envelope. A tangible item that the author was handing over. It was a symbol of *hope*.

This was my personal project that I developed and I called it 'Find My Story'. I wrote the short story inside the envelopes and devised the concept of randomly distributing them. I believed that my festive fairy tale would find just one person who needed a positive message at a challenging time of the year. It became so much more. Over the next five years I wrote two more stories. An army of volunteers helped me distribute thousands of envelopes across the globe. But most importantly, I was inundated with profound and moving responses from people who found a random envelope and had the curiosity to open it. Responses like these:

- *"Found one of these and I'd be lying if I said I didn't break down in tears."*
- *"I can't begin to say how much this gift has meant to me."*
- *"It's impossible to describe how this story made me feel."*

Throughout the entire period I was writing and distributing these positive stories, I was suffering from relentless depression, anxiety and negative thinking. The struggles my characters overcame were a direct reflection of the ones that consumed me. *And no one knew.* Not my friends, family or colleagues, not even my wife. It was my secret shame. A state of mind that I equated with failure and could never imagine sharing.

I continued to distribute my envelopes every December for the next five years. The positive responses provided me with a temporary boost to my emotional wellbeing, and I desperately clung to the message of hope I so gladly distributed to others. *It was not enough.* My defensive fortress of cognitive behavioural therapy

(CBT), mindfulness and yoga was crumbling under the relentless power of my negative thoughts. *Nothing* worked.

So, in 2019, I made a decision. That would be the last year distributing my envelopes. My depression had won. The bright beacon of positivity my annual adventure had provided was finally being consumed by my negativity. And worst of all, it felt like a permanent shift in my personality. A fixed state of mind that would accompany me for the rest of my life. I saw no way out.

And then, less than three weeks after I distributed the last of my envelopes, I discovered *The Kind Mind Method*. It seemed to arrive from nowhere: a bewildering and life-changing gift that was teleported directly into my mind. At first, I greedily accepted this gift without question; its origin felt almost irrelevant compared to the positive changes I received. But as time went by, my curiosity emerged. I wanted to understand *why* and *how* this had happened to me. I reached back through the years, trying to find a specific event or moment that provided my inspiration.

As it turned out, the answer was obvious.

For the five years I ran my project, I'd been overwhelmed by the support and help of others. Friends, family and strangers alike came together to help distribute my envelopes and spread a positive message across the country – for no other reason than to do a good deed. Each year, I received hundreds of messages from people describing the challenges of life and how this random message had somehow found them at *just* the right time. How the gift I distributed truly meant something to them and they would carry it with them forever. How they desperately needed that reminder that hope lived within them.

There is no doubt in my mind. This was my inspiration. These envelopes. These people. Their hope.

All of it, from a simple act of *kindness*.

1

INTRODUCTION

A brief introduction,
a little bit about depression
and how to use this book.

THE KIND MIND METHOD

Do you *worry* about what you have said? Or mentally dissect your conversations to analyse whether there could have been anything offensive hidden within? Maybe you worry about what you *might* say. Or actually, maybe you worry about the fact you feel like you have *nothing* to say? Do you worry about your job? Or your family? Or maybe you worry about the fact you worry too much? Or whether your forgetfulness is Alzheimer's rather than just the result of an overworked mind trying to deal with your worry. Possibly your worries have merged into one swirling mass of worry that has now taken residence in your stomach and rejoices in reminding you each morning to do some more worrying.

If you answered yes to any of the above, then I believe this book can help you. And I believe this because just a few years ago, I worried about pretty much *everything*. In fact, I worried so much that the world around me, the people around me, simply faded into the background. They became the muted voices that were unable to compete with the burning creativity of my own negative thoughts.

And then, on 10 January 2020, I went away for a weekend with friends, and *everything changed.* Over those two days a simple thought process emerged within me that completely wiped away my worry. Before the weekend, I had no control of my thoughts. They were unstoppable. As I returned home on the Sunday evening, my thoughts were my own. I could decide where my imagination would take me. I had a *choice.* A better world to explore. A brighter option than the dark shadows of negativity I had been immersed in. And that choice gave me freedom. And with that, the weight of my depression and the frantic buzzing of my anxiety were instantly destroyed.

This was not the gentle nudge of CBT or the brief respite of meditation. This was a profound, lasting and bewildering change within me that occurred over just two days. *And it is this simple thought process, this transformational change, that I want to share with you.* A process that will:

- Provide you with an endless supply of positive thoughts that you will *actively want to chase.*
- Encourage you to step forward and turn these positive thoughts into *real-world outcomes.*
- Provide a mental safe space that will *protect you* from negative thinking.

In the pages that follow, I will walk you through clear steps on how to integrate this process into every aspect of your life. And that last statement is key: into *every* aspect of your life. You may not believe me yet, but this process is absolutely and fundamentally at the core of my personality now. I have adopted it entirely, and it is the foundation of me and my interaction with the wider world. It has walked with me every single day since the weekend I discovered it.

HOW WILL THIS BOOK HELP YOU?

There are two key reasons why I believe this book is different to *anything* else you may have read on this subject. Firstly, this is not a collection of anecdotes or a series of complex tips to deploy in a variety of circumstances. This is *one simple* thought process. One process that will take seconds to learn and is incredibly easy to use. Most importantly, it will harness the natural creativity that flows within you and allow you to deploy it in *any* situation life throws your way:

- **I AM WORRIED ABOUT THE FUTURE OR THE PAST:** use this process to immediately snap you back into the moment.
- **I AM CONSUMED WITH NEGATIVE THOUGHTS:** use this process to provide you with an alternative and better thought. A thought that you will actively want to pursue.
- **I AM ANXIOUS DURING SOCIAL SITUATIONS:** this process will encourage you to engage with others and provide you with conversational fuel in the moment.

- **I HAVE A CHALLENGING SITUATION THAT I CAN'T COPE WITH:** use this thought process to reframe your problem.
- **I AM DISTANT FROM THOSE CLOSE TO ME:** there is simply nothing that will bring you back to your friends and family better than this thought process.

The second and most critical differentiator is *kindness*. For years, scientific studies have continuously demonstrated a clear link between kindness and mental wellbeing. Throughout that time, there has never been any unified mechanism to harness this power. *Until now.* This thought process is inspired by, and powered by, kindness to others. As we step through how to use this process, you will see how kindness draws you in and encourages you to engage with better and more positive thoughts. You will see clear examples of how the smallest and simplest of kind acts will enforce and energise the use of this process and provide you with continued protection from worry. And most importantly, I intend to convince you that this thought process will change you in ways you could never have imagined. The release from negative thinking, depression or anxiety is only the beginning. This simple thought process will encourage you to be a better person. A more sociable person. A kinder person.

This is *The Kind Mind Method.*

And now, my ask of you is simple. Why not try taking one of those negative *what if?* questions I suspect dominate so much of your thinking and apply it to this thought process. *What if it helps?* Just imagine. Before that January weekend away, I would have done anything to free myself from my thoughts. I never would have believed it to be possible. But it was. *And it is.*

depression

noun (unhappiness)

1. the state of feeling very unhappy and without hope for the future

This book is intended for anyone who wants to adopt a more positive outlook on life. It also provides an approach to manage negative thinking, as well as the subsequent depression and anxiety it can develop into. But these are broad terms that can be easily misinterpreted. Our minds are a universe of individual thoughts and complexity, and because of this, your definition of these terms may be very different from my own. Your *experience* of these terms will certainly be different. Whatever your problems are, I understand that they are indeed *yours.*

Within this section, though, I would like to touch upon some of the common threads that these terms all share. And the simplest and best way to do that is through my own experience. My *depression.* My *anxiety.* With this insight, you will be better able to apply the principles within this book. You will see where I was mentally and what elements of a worrisome mind we share. And as the thought process is revealed, I believe this understanding will help you recognise the steps *you* need to take towards a different way of thinking.

From an external perspective, I had no real reason to be depressed. I seemed to have it all: loving family, nice house, good job. Except I didn't. Not in my mind. I was consumed with negative thinking. Loving family: *what if someone gets ill?* Nice house: *what if I can't pay the mortgage?* Good job: *what if I get made redundant?* Even the brief recognition of my good fortune would usually be accompanied by guilt: *what reason do I have to be depressed? Look at some of the struggles other people have to face. I should be happy.*

No fear or worry, however ludicrous, was left unexplored.

It hadn't always been like this. For the vast majority of my previous forty-odd years, I had been generally happy, averagely positive about life, outgoing(ish) and rarely concerned with the inner machinations of my mind. It just worked. Most of the time. Then, at some indiscernible point in time and by degrees so small that I never noticed, that changed, and it didn't work anymore. My occasional worries had multiplied exponentially, and the lines between them became blurred. They were not individual worries to manage. Instead, they were an overwhelming sea of worry that I was swimming in. And I'd always been a *really* crap swimmer.

One thing that did remain constant, both before and during my mental struggles, was the amount of time I spent within my own mind. I'd always been a daydreamer. What if I won the lottery? What if I could fly? What if lightsabers were real? What if...? It used to be a world of possibilities, and I loved to explore every corner. And these thoughts drove an outcome. Work problems I could solve. Ideas I could implement. Places I could go and things I could do. Time spent internally was a familiar place to me, but it was a good place, and I craved the time to indulge my thoughts.

The change within me may have taken time, but it was laughably simple. A binary switch that turned my creative mind from positive to negative and changed *everything.* Instead of my thoughts being powered by hope and positivity, they became contaminated with worry and fear. I don't know why. Or how. But the insidious emotions were unstoppable.

Positive thoughts were replaced with catastrophic worries about an imaginary future or regrets from the past. My creative mind remained as frantic and productive as ever, though. Small seeds of doubt would grow into whole worlds of worry. And everything was powered by the same simple question: *what if?* But the question had changed. No longer was this the springboard for inspiration and ideas. It felt like the deceitful grip of a fairy tale witch luring me down a dark, lonely path that would lead only to despair.

I continued to spend hours every day locked within my mind. My negative thoughts were intoxicating and relentless. At some level I knew how destructive they were, but like an addict, I just couldn't stop. Each thought fuelling the next. Building and consuming. When I did occasionally step out of my internal world, I would be drained and tired, all my energy spent on the negative thoughts that had been bombarding my mind. Worse still, I would have nothing to show for the creative effort and energy I was exerting. These ludicrous worries were my hidden shame that I vowed *never* to share with anyone.

I was locked in a mental prison of my own making. And it felt like there was no escape.

In practical terms there are many symptoms we tie to depression: forgetfulness, indecision, anger, social isolation and many others. For me, these were indeed present and correct. In the time it would take me to get up from my seat and go to the fridge, I could forget what I'd wanted to get. I could spend hours agonising over the wording of an email and then immediately regret my choices the second I hit send. I would get furious over the smallest of indiscretions. I would take any opportunity to drop out of a social get-together. My list did indeed go on and on.

I was so consumed with my internal thinking that I simply had no spare brain capacity to deal with anything else. My mind was running at 100 mph but going absolutely nowhere. Worst of all, I still remembered the positive, creative world of *before,* and I would often try to recapture those hours, those moments, where ideas would flow, thoughts would spark – *but nothing.* I was expending so much effort for so little return.

Finally, we come back to that word 'depression'. It means so much to so many. From an outsider's perspective, a label for someone who may be *a bit sad*; from an insider's point of view, a Jackson Pollock picture of a chaotic and confused mind. So personal to each of us. So difficult to describe. So hard to share.

I want to be crystal clear about what I mean by depression and what this thought process has helped me address. *Negative thinking.* The toxic thoughts that cause so much damage. Not being able to control these thoughts that rampage into – and then through – your mind. The inability to control them and the catastrophic repercussions they can have. The *what if?* questions that creep in and interrupt your sleep. The mental tap that you simply can't turn off. Or for me, being locked inside my creative mind with no escape from the world of worry I was building. *This was my depression.*

Using The Kind Mind Method has utterly transformed my thinking. It provides me with a safe space to let my thoughts roam. An outlet for my creative energy. And most importantly, when I *see* a negative thought, *I now have a true choice.* I believe this is the fundamental factor that makes this process work so well. When I was depressed, I knew that once I had dispensed with a negative thought, there would be another waiting eagerly in the wings. Not anymore. I now have a *better* thought that I can choose. A thought that actively drives me to engage with the wider world. A thought that helps me see my negative thinking for the poison it truly is.

The mental switch that caused my depression has been flipped. I am using my imagination with a positive foundation to build upon. It feels so simple. Once more I can explore creative possibilities, ideas and thoughts. Once more I can ask the question that drove so many of my dreams and passions without fear: *what if...?*

HOW TO USE THIS BOOK

1. CONTINUE TO DO WHAT YOU NEED TO DO

This thought process is the single most powerful cognitive tool I encountered when I was struggling with depression and anxiety. Nothing else worked for me. And it is this knowledge that relentlessly drives me onward to spread this message to others. But my goal is to provide you with a tool for your mental toolbox. It is not to deter you from alternative or existing forms of treatment.

CBT may not have been enough to stop my depression, but it helped me understand that my negative thoughts were truly negative. Equally, I believe exercise plays a huge role in supporting my mental health; alone, it may not have been enough to pull me from my negative world, but I understand that it is an important piece of the overall puzzle, and it remains a solid foundation for my positive thoughts to build on.

Whatever you do, whatever you take, please continue to do so. I am not trying to *convert* you, and my confidence is not a slight on any other approach to mental health treatment. I believe, I hope, that this book can provide you with an answer to your problems. But I also understand that the true answer is, simply, *whatever works for you.*

2. FINISH THE BOOK

The Kind Mind Method is extremely simple, and in practical terms, it will take you seconds to learn. And because of this, you may be tempted to read Chapter 3, where I reveal the exact nature of this process, and then casually throw the book over your shoulder and skip merrily into the distance to benefit from the promised changes. *I urge you not to do so.* Not yet, anyway. I would strongly suggest you finish this book before trying to adopt the process outlined within it. There is a broad context to understand: how and why the process can help in a range of different situations. Without this background, this understanding, I fear you may not fully embrace the approach and, therefore, not truly realise all of the benefits.

3. KEEP IT TO YOURSELF

For at least the first week you are implementing this thought process, I would suggest you limit the number of people you talk to about it. The mechanism that is used to shift yourself away from negative thinking can be easily misinterpreted by others, and this can directly impact the outcome. Once you understand its use, and the change within you, then you'll be able to share with anyone and everyone as you see fit.

4. KEEP IT SIMPLE

To help you quickly adopt The Kind Mind Method, I have tried to make this book as simple as possible.

I'll start by taking you briefly back in time to the moment this thought process revealed itself to me, before jumping straight into its usage and providing practical tips on how to integrate it into your daily life. We'll then spend some time looking at both the scientific and practical reasons behind why this process can deliver such a transformational change. Accompanying all of this will be real-world examples showing how The Kind Mind Method has been used to provide inspiration and guidance in many different situations.

The last section of this book will provide you with key steps to implement this thought process and covers:

- **ADOPTING** a kind mind
- **USING** your kind mind
- **ENHANCING** your kind mind

It is my hope that by the end of this book, you will understand *why* this thought process works so well at stopping depression, anxiety and negative thinking. You will know *how* to use it on a daily basis and to manage any stressful situation. And most importantly, you will realise how *simple* it is. How it takes almost no effort. All because you will be chasing a better thought. A *kinder* thought.

2

THE WEEKEND

On 10 January 2020, I went away for a weekend with friends. Over the course of that weekend, The Kind Mind Method emerged within me, and I returned home on the Sunday evening a completely different person. Even now, years later, I still struggle to comprehend the profound and lasting change that happened in such a short space of time.

Throughout this book I will talk you through how you can benefit from this thought process. But for a brief moment, I would like to step back in time and take you on a journey to the Yorkshire Dales. A journey that changed my life. And the start of a journey that I believe could also change yours.

SURPRISE!

'Should we take the Alfa?' my wife, Clare, asked with a puppy-dog look of excitement that didn't come close to breaching the walls of anxiety I had constructed around myself.

'Err.' I tried to think of the exact words that would make the question – and the entire weekend ahead – disappear. I managed another distracted 'err' before walking off with an intent look on my face and hoping that if I couldn't skip the weekend, then at least I might be able to get my wife to stop pestering me to make a decision about the car for the next five minutes. I walked inside the house, the kids brushing past me in a bellow of noise and bustle of elbows, and made my way upstairs to sit on the bed for a moment. Thoughts danced erratically through my mind whilst anxiety and anger argued amongst themselves to determine who would win the battle for physical control of my body. I flicked my phone on and browsed through the news, Facebook and Twitter – anything to take my mind off the next couple of days and the painful ache that was growing in my stomach.

'What are you doing?' Clare shouted from downstairs.

The phone leapt from my hands, and I juggled it guiltily as if I'd been watching porn rather than mindlessly scanning articles on *The Guardian*.

'Coming,' I responded in my best 'everything-is-groovy' voice, instead of the 'why-don't-you-fuck-off-and-leave-me-alone' voice that was shrieking loudly in the back of my mind. Seemed anger had won the battle over anxiety after all.

'What were you doing?' she asked, looking irritated as I walked downstairs.

The truth – that I'd been aimlessly scrolling through the news on my phone to take my mind away from the weekend ahead – didn't really feel like the ideal precursor to a three-hour drive with my wife and kids, so I lied.

'I was just getting some stuff,' I replied, glad she didn't dig deeper into the response as I shuffled past her to grab my bag. It was 10 January 2020, and we were going away for a weekend with over twenty people for a friend's surprise fortieth birthday party. Clare was bouncing with excitement, every fibre of her extrovert body ready for days of chatting with friends and the opportunity to meet new people. I was overwhelmed and consumed with despair at the thought of going. I felt exhausted and tired from a Christmas break that only just seemed to have ended. In addition, I'd just returned from several days working away from home: four hours there, two nights in a Travelodge and four hours back, the whole time, my social anxiety reaching critical levels as I endeavoured to portray a veneer of normality to my work colleagues. I was drained, my tank felt empty and I just wanted to sit alone in a quiet room.

I also felt that the heavy weight that had taken residence in my stomach and the escalating tension and anxiety were building towards a tipping point. Years of hiding my feelings. Covering up the physical symptoms of sweating, nausea and numerous others I suffered to get through the day. The hours and hours of each day I would spend distant and within a dark world of negative thoughts that no end of CBT seemed able to contain. I truly felt I just wasn't going to be able to continue in the way I had been. I knew something had to change, and I feared the worst (as I always did). A breakdown? Time off work? Having to admit to my wife that I was **DEPRESSED**? All of the above?

Each time my mind turned to the weekend ahead, the tension in my body would ratchet up another level. The thought of forcing conversation with my friends when I felt as if I had nothing to say made me shrink further inwards. And thinking about the handful of strangers I would have to engage with caused a physical ache within me. All this while having to maintain the façade. Smile. Laugh. Try not to let my negative thoughts overwhelm me. Deflect questions back onto others to hide my inability to engage or interest people. I was good at it, although it always took effort. It was so tiring. I knew that drink would offer a welcome and temporary respite from the anxiety – and possibly see me through the nights. But the shadow of the morning would loom heavily; the black dog of despair always seemed meaner after a night of drinking.

'So, are we taking the Alfa?' Clare asked again. The mild exasperation in her tone told me she was getting as annoyed at my procrastination as I was at her for asking the question.

Even with my mentally impaired decision-making process, it should have been a simple question to answer. The Alfa was less than a month old, a sporty saloon that was a joy to drive. Clare obviously wanted to take it, and the boys were already sitting in the back seats and plugging headphones into their tablets for the journey ahead. There was just one problem: *the farm track.*

I had scanned through the directions to the accommodation, and as invitingly secluded as the farmhouse looked, there was an annoyingly obtuse reference to a lengthy farm track that took you from the main road to the actual house. As much as I scanned the reviews and every corner of the website, I could find no further details about the state of the track. Was it an extended driveway that we would breeze happily down? Or a bumpy track that my brand new and extremely low-bodied Alfa Romeo would flounder on? The pressure was building intensely within me to respond. On one side, I knew Clare wanted to take the car, and being the eternally optimistic person she was, she would no more understand my reservations than she would understand Russian. On the other side was *the farm track*. The off-road track I was building in my mind that would surely devour and damage the Alfa before leaving us stranded in the dark.

'Well?' she asked again, now looking at me as if I was a total idiot. A not unfamiliar look in those days.

'Alright, yes, let's take it if you want to,' I said, grabbing the keys and getting into the car. I knew Clare had no idea whatsoever why I was being irritable. Internally I was seething, my irrational mind furious at my wife for forcing me to take my own car. The catastrophic outcomes were beginning to form in my mind even before we started moving. In my broken mind, I knew one thing for certain: it would be all her fault if we got stuck.

I don't believe in fate. I don't think there's a bigger picture or a pre-ordained path for us to follow. I do believe that small events can have staggering implications, though, and less than two minutes after we set off, Clare read a message that, I think, changed my life forever. We'd only just pulled out of our cul-de-sac when her phone buzzed with the notification.

'Looks like Ben and Emily have arrived,' she said.

I ignored her entirely. My mind was on a muddy track in North Yorkshire, with two kids crying in the back seat and the car beached on a jagged rock that had ripped the underside of the engine to pieces.

'Oooh, looks like the road is actually a bit bumpy,' she said, reading the message and then nonchalantly putting the phone away as if nothing was amiss. My spider-senses exploded. I knew Clare's blind optimism meant that nothing anyone could have texted would have made her think taking the Alfa was a problem.

'What did they say?' I shouted.

'Err, OK, shouty. Hang on,' she said, getting her phone back out. *'Nearly left the bottom of my car on the farm track! It's like an obstacle course – be prepared!'* she said, reading from the phone. 'I'm sure it'll be fine; he's probably exaggerating.'

I'd been crippled with indecision for years. Almost all decisions I'd made would be wrangled over for hours, sometimes even days. We'd built an extension two years earlier and I'd almost had a breakdown as my mind had fallen into an infinite decision loop for days about what type of windows we should get. I hadn't been decisive about anything for years. *Until now.*

'We're taking the Honda,' I said, swinging the car into a side street and turning around. I gave Clare no choice. Her brief look of annoyance simply bounced off my surprisingly out-of-character decisiveness. And right then, even as I managed to undermine my confidence by carrying out an awkward seven-point manoeuvre, I turned both my car and my life around.

Twenty minutes later I was driving our slightly battered – and most importantly, four-wheel drive – Honda CR-V down the same road. The kids had barely noticed the transition, a minor blip in their periphery vision and a brief interlude in their tablet-viewing time.

Clare was accepting, even though I knew she thought I was overreacting. I was simply relieved.

One of the many weights had been lifted from my body, and as we drove back down the same road we'd been on just minutes ago, I almost managed a smile. I hadn't changed my mind about the whole weekend, but the worry that I knew would have consumed the drive had been completely removed. My mind felt spacious, briefly open to new thoughts rather than crammed full of chaos. Through my own confident and positive actions, the weight of worry had vanished. As we hit the city boundary and merged onto the two-hour trudge of single carriageway, caravans and tractors that had to be navigated to exit Norfolk, I wasn't excited or happy about the weekend ahead. But for just a moment, I wasn't worried.

About two hours into the journey, the change within me edged closer. As I'd been left with only one job to prepare for the weekend ahead – sort the kid's tech out for the car journey – it came as no great surprise to anyone when both of their batteries ran out with about an hour and a half left to go. Usually, a long car journey would have been an ideal opportunity for me to create an imaginary world of fear in my mind, but as more and more people arrived at the farmhouse before us, the positive freedom I'd gained from my earlier actions continued to strengthen. Every message to our chat group seemed to increase the reputation of the rugged, rock-strewn and muddy track as a fearsome beast we'd all have to face upon arrival.

*'Holy ****, there's no way we'll ever be able to get out of here again!'* said Clare reading out the latest message on her phone from another arrival at the farm, mouthing the obscenity to shield the kids.

'Who's that one from?' I asked, eager to hear further confirmation of the confident decision I'd made earlier in the journey.

'Err, some of Bryan's friends, we don't know them,' she said, holding the phone up.

I glanced over, not at all interested in their names and simply revelling in the ever-increasing affirmation that my U-turn had made perfect sense. *'Holy shit, there's no way we'll ever be able to get out of here again!'* I read, slowly and loudly to truly hammer home how correct I'd been about swapping the cars. I wasn't sure whether the punch on the arm from Clare was for swearing in front of the kids or for just being irritating.

I found that the situation had cleared some of the noise that typically filled my mind and, for the briefest time, I was able to observe the moment. I was driving through beautiful countryside on our way to a North

Yorkshire Farm, with my amazing wife beside me and my most precious cargo sitting in the back getting bored because I hadn't charged their tablets. I started to take in my surroundings, both inside and out. My youngest son, Brodie, was swinging his leg and gently tapping the back of my seat, either out of boredom or just to highlight his thoughts about my tablet-charging capabilities. Dexter was gazing happily out the window. It was this rare moment of respite that I believe allowed the change within me to evolve.

'What's mutton?' Dexter asked from the back seat. Having two young boys, both under the age of ten, does mean that I was used to strange and often nonsensical questions. But even for them, this one felt particularly random.

'Why?' Clare asked before I was able to.

'The pub back there was called The Shoulder of Mutton. I was just wondering what mutton was.'

'It's a type of sheep,' I replied.

'Oh. OK. Is that like a lamb, then?'

'Sort of,' I said, painfully aware that the further I went down this conversational cul-de-sac it would become obvious that I wasn't entirely sure what mutton was. *Was it just an old sheep?* 'It's an older sheep,' I said in the best 'Dad-knows-everything-so-please-don'task-anymore-questions' voice I could muster. I was hoping this would be enough to quench their thirst for further knowledge on the topic.

'Like, how old?' Brodie piped up, suddenly expressing a keen interest in all things sheep related.

'Sort of older than sheep.'

'I thought you said it was a type of sheep?' Dexter asked, looking confused.

'Yeah, Dad. You did,' Brodie responded in a rare moment of solidarity with his brother, something they usually saved for arguing with me.

'No, I meant older than a lamb.' Out of the corner of my eye, I could see Clare laughing.

'Would you like me to Google it?' she asked.

'Yeah,' came the shout from the back seats.

'Look, you don't need to Google it,' I said. 'A lamb is a young sheep and mutton is an older sheep. It's not difficult.'

The boys paused to absorb my statement.

'So, if a lamb is a young sheep. And mutton is an old sheep. What's a sheep, then?' asked Dexter.

I was pretty sure he was just taking the piss now. I decided it was time to change the subject.

'What would you call your pub?' I asked. It was a general question thrown over my shoulder with the simple goal of distracting them from my ignorance of all things sheep related. Brodie was first back with an immediate and confident answer.

'I would call my pub The Farty Bob.'

We both burst out laughing. 'Clearly named after Daddy,' Clare said before either of the kids could say the same.

'Oi! And what about you, Dex?'

Always the thinker, Dexter leaned back and pondered for a few minutes. Finally, he responded. 'Well, it would probably be owned by me, Henley and Luca, so I think we'd call it... The Crazy Loons,' he said, clearly happy with his choice.

I glanced in the mirror and looked at my world smiling at me from the back seats. So often our time together was through the chatter of my mind. Their questions would feel like interruptions to the fantasy world of fear I would be creating, my answers clipped and short as I'd be distracted by my negative thoughts. Here, now, through my simple question, I had made them *smile.* I was smiling. Clare was smiling. *I had done that.* Yes, they had made us laugh through their unique and classic pub names, but I asked that question. I brought about that laughter. It may sound small, simple and stupid to an outsider, but it wasn't to me, and something changed for the remainder of the journey. I actively shifted my thoughts outward. Rather than spending hours building elaborate and negative scenarios in my mind, I focussed on my children. No longer did I drift back into my mind at the first gap in the conversation. Instead, my thoughts turned to those smiles. To The Farty Bob and The Crazy Loon. How my simple question had brought them about. How we had laughed. How we had smiled. *How I could repeat that feeling.*

At each pause in the conversation, I would actively think to myself, *how can I recreate their smiles?* I asked questions. I answered more questions. I said silly things, and they said even sillier things. Never once did my thoughts turn to the weekend ahead and my fear and anxiety. Money, redundancy, divorce and death, usually my trusty companions for all long journeys regardless of the company, never once lingered beyond a momentary flicker. It was a revelation. It was truly unlike anything I had experienced for years. I was actively engaging in conversation rather than being frustrated at having someone interrupt my internal monologue.

I recognise that someone who does not suffer with depression may read these paragraphs with confusion. Surely all I was doing was having a chat? But here's the difference. Every conversation I'd had over the past five years had been accompanied by the self-doubting background chatter of my mind. Every question was an interruption. Every smile was forced. Every action was done on autopilot while my mind burned brightly with negative thoughts.

So I knew this was something different. I was filling the gaps in my mind, not with worry, but with one simple question. Repeating it over and over again. A constant question to myself that drove discussion and laughter. *How can I make them smile?* I was forcing my thoughts outwards, flooding my mind. It was a relentless surge of forward momentum, one single thought that completely smothered the nipping voice of negativity. My confidence grew as the conversation evolved, and fewer and fewer gaps needed to be filled as the journey progressed. To this day I don't truly understand the thought process that led me there, but I was, for what felt like the first time in a very, very long time, happy.

We arrived at the farm just after 8 pm. By that point we knew what to expect from *the farm track*, although that didn't stop my enthusiastic commentary highlighting each hole, ditch and drain that would surely have stopped my Alfa Romeo in its tracks. The Honda glided down the farm track, and when we reached the farmyard, the kids leapt from the back seats as if they'd been released from jail. I stretched and yawned as I stepped out and surveyed our surroundings. It was dark, but the silhouette from the rolling Yorkshire hillsides loomed all around us like thick curtains. Light from the two farmhouses splashed over the bonnet of the car and voices spilled out from the door nearest to us.

I paused, suddenly aware of a strange sensation flowing through me. My thinking over the last hour or so had taken me away from constructing a negative narrative about the weekend ahead, and I felt a glimmer of optimism. I wouldn't say I was excited, but it felt as if there was the possibility of a good time to be had. Instinctively I knew this was the result of my actions in the car. I couldn't quite put into words what had happened, except that I had engaged in a tangible action: thinking about how I could fill the quiet moments of my mind. This thought process had overwritten the space I normally would have allocated to negative thinking and enabled a positive engagement with my family. I knew I wanted to continue whatever it was I was doing.

We walked into the farm and there was a flurry of noise, handshakes and hugs. Conversations, kids and dogs swarmed around me, and for a brief moment, my fear and anxiety fluttered at the chaos I had walked into. I hated these situations – the introductions, the noise, the half-conversations as I tried to focus on practical tasks such as unloading the car and getting the kids sorted. I was always able to portray an outwardly sociable exterior: my defences were honed to deflect and distract, and no one would ever have guessed that I had anxiety pulsing through me. But before my thoughts actively engaged in building a wall of worry, I mentally went back to the car and the thought process that had transformed the latter part of the journey. I took that thinking and brought it into the room with me and towards the crowd of people. I didn't yet have the clarity that I've developed over time. There was intent, though. An intent to change my thinking, to reach out, to maintain forward and outward momentum whenever negative thoughts threatened to pivot inwards.

As the night progressed, it evolved and became like a game. The kitchen began to bulge at the seams and I relentlessly filled my thoughts with how I could positively engage with each new arrival. It was a clear and distinct mechanism that I was using with each and every person I met. Friend or stranger, my thoughts would reach outward, and I would repeat, over and over again, one simple question. *How can I make them smile?*

That night was the best I'd had in years. There was a freedom in my words and actions that I would never have dreamed possible mere hours earlier. All my fear and anxiety was washed away by positive thoughts as my thinking shifted into a more proactive frame of mind. I laughed. Not just a physical action weighed down by the fog of my depression. This was laughter with true passion and joy, a feeling that ran through my entire body rather than something I was forced to paint on my face. I spoke to strangers. When there was a gap in the conversation, instead of filling the silence with internal worries about the situation, I focussed on topics for discussion. I actively considered how I could engage with people. *How can I make them smile?* It was a consistent internal thought that drove me forward and that never once allowed negative thoughts to gain traction.

I spoke to friends late into the night. We talked about life, love, the universe and, if I remember correctly, my friend Colm's weird-looking ear: deep, important and equally frivolous conversations that only alcohol and good company can create. The anchor of my negative thoughts was gone. I felt, however briefly, *free*. This was a sensation I had all but given up hope of ever achieving again. It felt like the Alexander of old. As I crept up the creaky stairs in the early hours of the morning, I was almost in tears at the intensity and clarity of the experience. I had thought this carefree person had gone forever, and here he was, stumbling up the stairs of an isolated farm in the middle of nowhere. *Very* drunk. *Very* happy.

For many years I had relied heavily on alcohol to support and guide me through almost all social occasions. Nothing seemed to calm the beating heart of anxiety like the first glass of wine. Nothing would add a confident voice to my fragile thoughts like finishing the first bottle of wine. So, the next morning, with less than four hours' sleep, two children bouncing happily on the bed and a headache that I knew no amount of paracetamol would appease, I had to face a stark question: *how much of the night before was the alcohol?* Had it just been some supercharged and drunken frenzy of confidence? An inspired moment brought about by circumstance and red wine? I thought as hard as my damaged brain could think, and the simple answer was *no*. I truly believed that this was something different. There was a clear thought process, an intent to change, that had started well before any alcohol had passed my lips. This had been all me. I was sure of it.

We stayed in bed for a couple of hours before the bustle and banging from downstairs rose to a level we couldn't ignore any longer. I walked nervously into the kitchen, my hangover bringing my anxiety back. I watched the people swirl around me as my thoughts began to turn inward. A realisation was growing within me. What had happened the night before – the question I'd been asking myself to fill the gap of self-doubt and fear in my mind – I simply couldn't sustain through the hangover. For a moment, I had thought I'd discovered something special, a change within me that I could harness and build upon to improve my life. But as I sat in the kitchen, my heart thundering and my mind clouded from alcohol and tiredness, I just couldn't seem to dredge up the mental energy to replicate my thought process. To reach outward and attempt to make people smile. *It just felt too hard.*

Maybe later, maybe it's something I can use some of the time? Maybe just on nights out? I didn't want to give up entirely; there was *something* there. I surveyed the room, considering if there was any way I could reignite the spark and push my mind to fill the gap before negative thinking did it for me. I just couldn't do it... not the same way I had the night before. I had flooded my mind with that one question, constantly looking for ways I could positively engage with people and make them smile. That simply wasn't there this morning. I didn't feel as if I had the energy, willpower or confidence.

I took one last glance around the room. People bustled. Talked. Smiled. I watched as an outsider, ready and resigned to once again take my role on the periphery, a spectator watching the weekend pass me by as the actors enjoyed their moment in the spotlight.

My eyes landed on Emily, standing alone at the kitchen sink washing dishes. Emily was partially deaf, a challenge that she seemingly shrugged off with a confidence and grace I could only dream of replicating. I knew how difficult the rambling and incoherent conversations could become for her to interpret as the night progressed and alcohol flowed, but she never stepped back from the challenge. A sudden thought occurred to me. A thought so simple yet so perfect. A thought that would add another dimension to the mental process that was forming in my mind. One more simple question. A question that even in my hungover state I felt capable of answering. I stepped up to the kitchen sink.

'Hi Emily, can I help you?' I asked.

Right then, my life changed forever.

Those two questions filled almost every waking moment of the remaining two days. I was in awe at how they utterly changed my engagement with everyone around me. I truly enjoyed the weekend. I felt happier and more confident than I had done in years. This was not a gradual change; it was a light-switch moment that brought about a freedom and calm within my mind that I had long ago given up hope of achieving. The two elements, almost plucked at random from time and circumstance, formed a perfect symmetry to quieten the angry voice in my mind and remove the painful ache in my stomach. I shifted my thoughts from negative thinking to questions about how I could engage with the wider world and the people around me. I proactively filled the gaps by considering others and not myself. I faced into anxious situations by considering what I *would* do rather than worrying about what *might happen*.

Two simple questions that I repeated to myself over and over. ***How can I help them? How can I make them smile?***

3

TWO QUESTIONS

Is it really that simple?
Spoiler alert: it is.

WHAT IS IT?

I suspect that when I explain The Kind Mind Method, many of you will be surprised by the simplicity. This simplicity, though, is one of the key elements that allows this process to have such a broad and deep impact. There is little to learn, some basic words that will provide a lighthouse of focus in the stormy sea of your mind. But do not judge the simplicity as something negative. The simplicity, the ease of access, makes the process easier to adopt. To channel my inner Yoda: where we have complexity, it can often lead to confusion. Confusion leads to frustration, and frustration results in rejection. In this instance, simpler really is better.

The words you are going to learn will provide an ethos, an outlook that you can take into *every* moment of the day: from the chatter of your 4 am mind lying awake in bed, to the panic of social engagements and work. The core principle is a set of two questions that you repeat to yourself over and over. These aren't just platitudes to boost your confidence. They have two distinct perspectives:

- **PROTECTION:** the questions will provide alternative thoughts that you can engage with. These will all be positive thoughts that you will be motivated to indulge, and most importantly, they will provide you with a *safe mental space that protects you from negative thinking.*

- **ENGAGEMENT:** the questions will challenge you to engage with the wider world. They will *trigger your internal creativity* to encourage you to look for ways to *engage with other people* rather than focussing on the fear of what you may say or do.

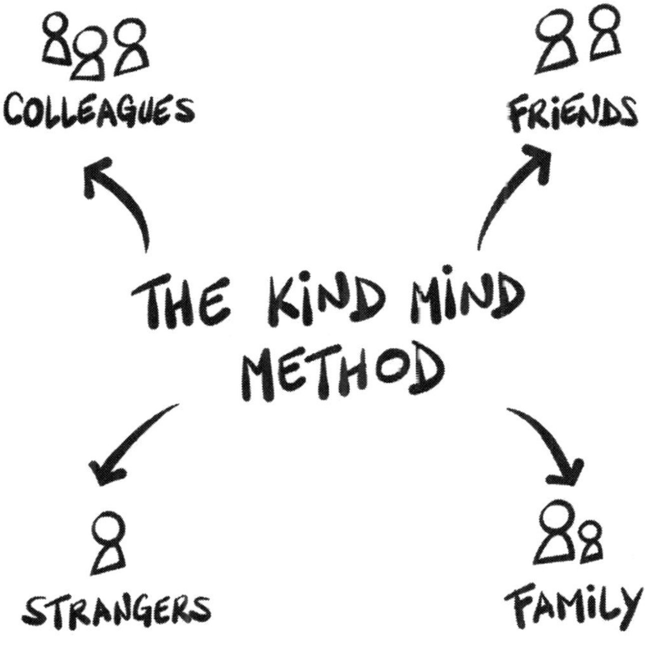

Throughout the next section, we will explore how the protection and engagement that is provided by these simple questions can be used to deal with all aspects of negative thinking. Although there are many different situations to explore, the implementation remains the same. This familiarity will help you absorb the words deeper into your daily life, and over time it will become effortless. You don't need to remember anything. You don't need to spend time out of your day practising it. You just do it – and see the results.

HOW EXACTLY DOES IT WORK?

The Kind Mind Method is two sentences. More explicitly, two questions, that you will repeat internally to yourself. These questions will become central to every action and thought that you have from this point onwards. You will repeat them every morning, you will repeat them every time you have a negative thought, you will repeat them as you are speaking to friends, family or colleagues, you will repeat them when you get angry, you will repeat them when you are alone with your thoughts and you will repeat them last thing at night. The questions could not be easier or simpler:

- **HOW CAN I HELP THEM?**
- **HOW CAN I MAKE THEM SMILE?**

Repeat them quickly, and repeat them over and over: ***How can I help them? How can I make them smile? How can I help them? How can I make them smile? How can I help them? How can I make them smile?***

There are no other words, no other activities to practice each day. These two simple questions are *everything.* I have repeated them hundreds of times every day, and that familiarity — that sense of protection and guidance that they provide — is a significant part of why this process works so well.

Within seconds, you will remember the words and be able to repeat them, but they never become repetitive; each time you use them, they will have a different purpose, a different context. At times, the words will blur, with little meaning beyond a protective shield to stop your thoughts from roaming through the dark corridors of your mind like Jack Nicholson bumbling through the Overlook Hotel looking for scary stuff. At other times, you will focus on the questions and your thoughts will be directed outwards. ***How can I help them? How can I make them smile?*** Friends, family, colleagues or strangers, the questions apply to *any and all.* They force you to step out of your internal world, providing a tangible activity that not only takes you away from negative thinking but actively helps you engage with the wider world in a different way.

Like browsing the internet with no particular purpose, you will roam and come across people in your vicinity, family members and friends you may not have seen for years and actively pose these questions to yourself. ***How can I help them? How can I make them smile?*** What could you do to help them? Anything? A simple gesture or a grand plan? How could you make them smile? A joke? A story? Maybe it's even just starting a conversation?

Where before I would become lost in my own thoughts, at home or work, I am now pulled outwards, and many of the conversations I start, even with my closest family, have their genesis within this simple thought process. I have also spoken or engaged with hundreds of strangers because of these words. However small the interaction, it is always positive, always intended to illicit a smile or help them in some small way. This may have been after hours of simply repeating the words before finally coming across a brief smile or a door held open for a stranger.

Think about it: *what is the best use of your time and energy?* Worrying about what *might* happen in the future or asking yourself how you can help someone close to you or make them smile? The questions are so broad that they can be applied to *any* situation. Worried about meeting a group of friends? Simply repeat the words over and over again while focussing on the people and the event you fear. Anxiety is washed away by the practical question you are trying to address.

Consumed with negative thoughts? ***How can I help them? How can I make them smile?*** Over and over, make a choice to focus your mental energy on answering the questions. The negative thoughts fall away as your creative problem-solving kicks in and your mind pivots to a *positive* thought. Although the questions can be used in any situation and applied to any audience, they do have a very specific purpose: to direct *your thinking* outwards. Move *you* away from your internal world of negative thoughts and help *you* engage with the world. This step is *everything*. It will change *everything*. I couldn't stop myself from being consumed with utterly ridiculous and irrelevant thoughts. They bombarded me. They controlled me. No more, though. No more.

Within days you will begin to reap the benefits of the mental freedom it provides. *Yes*, most of your thoughts will be the repetition of these words. And *yes*, this may seem a bit crazy at first. A bit daft, or silly. But no more ridiculous than any of the thoughts you were previously having. Take a step back and consider the negative thinking, the anger, the depression and the anxiety that have been cluttering your mind. Toxic thoughts that can spiral out of control for hours or days. Would you not do anything to have control over these? Is it so difficult to simply repeat the same words over and over again? *I don't think so.* Remember, these words are important. You may be in a room full of strangers, searching outwardly to understand how you can help others, or in bed alone, warding off negative thoughts. But they are the *same* words, the *same* reassurance, *always* there for you whenever you need them. Speak them strongly in your mind. Feel the words. They have meaning; they are your guide to becoming the person you aspire to be.

HOW MIGHT THIS WORK ON A TYPICAL DAY?

When I wake in the morning my first thought will be the two questions. ***How can I help them? How can I make them smile?*** My focus, like my sleep-shrouded mind, will be blurry and indistinct. At this stage, the words are simply a positive intention with no particular target: a distraction from the fear and anxiety that would often fill my mind about the day ahead.

After breakfast, as my mind starts to generate Weetabix-fuelled negative thoughts, I ask myself the questions. ***How can I help them? How can I make them smile?*** They immediately shift me from negative thinking, and my focus drifts onto my family, who are fluttering around me. I step out of my mind and into the preschool chaos that I'd been oblivious to. I consider my wife, my children, and I repeat the questions. As I watch the hustle and bustle, I continue to repeat the words, finally noticing that my son can't find his shoes; I see an opportunity to help, and we begin trying to sort through the shoe-mountain in the cupboard under the stairs.

Mid-morning, I am battered by a meteor shower of negative thoughts and anxiety about a meeting later in the day. I recognise the possibility of being consumed for hours by the catastrophic consequences that *could* occur from the meeting. My social anxiety kicks in, and immediately I am swamped with fear that my nerves will consume me in the meeting. I repeat the words. ***How can I help them? How can I make them smile?*** I focus on the people in the meeting and consider different ways I can engage directly with them. My mind switches to a problem-solving mode. My fear drifts away as I am actively thinking about the meeting. I note down two questions that I want to ask one of the senior leaders and make a mental note to tell them an anecdote from my weekend. Each time my anxiety flutters, I repeat the words and, once more, face directly *into* the situation.

That night I go to the gym for a one-hour HIT session. Where my mind would previously have had an hour to bathe in negative thoughts, I proactively fill the mental space by repeating the process. ***How can I help them? How can I make them smile?*** I focus on the people surrounding me: *all strangers*. Each time I have a mental gap, a point where I feel my thoughts are drifting towards negativity, I repeat the words and continue to search the room. With minutes of the session left, I notice the man next to me has the same trainers I do. I comment on this to him. We talk briefly. *He smiles.*

I return from the gym and put the kids to bed. I potter around the kitchen and my wife comes in. I repeat the words and focus all my energy on her. ***How can I help them? How can I make them smile?*** I ask a simple question about her day. I continue to repeat the process, searching for ways to engage, ways to help her, make her smile. I ask more questions and we talk for over an hour.

As I lie in bed waiting for the deluge of thoughts to arrive, I repeat the words over and over again. They fill my mind and, much like the morning, I repeat the words with little focus, my mind flipping through people and situations to consider how the questions may apply to them. ***How can I help them? How can I make them smile?*** I fall asleep thinking that I need to buy my nephew a birthday present.

A VERY IMPORTANT POINT

Throughout the pages of this book, I will continually urge you to step out of your internal world and take the mental leap to translate your positive thoughts into a physical action. However small or inconsequential these actions may seem, seeing the real-world impact of the questions will provide fuel for the ongoing use of this process. More than that, seeing a tangible outcome will make it easier for you to choose this positive option over the negative thoughts that may have previously cluttered your mind.

There is a critical caveat to this statement, though. ***There should be no pressure or burden placed upon you by these two questions.*** Yes, push yourself to act on them. Embrace the external outlook that the constant repetition will embed within you. Even if it's just a simple smile to a stranger or a question to your partner, you will reap the rewards. But you should feel no disappointment or failure in the moments where you do *not* translate your thoughts into direct actions. There will always be other opportunities, and if you have been asking these questions and engaging directly with a creative thought, then you have achieved the desired result.

Remember, the sole purpose of this book, and the outcome you are striving to achieve, is a shift in *your* internal thoughts. It's about helping *you*, not others.

Consider this simple example. I am standing in the queue at my local supermarket. A micro-moment of downtime where I would typically rummage through the dark corners of my mind to find some negative thoughts to explore. Instead, I ask the questions. ***How can I help them? How can I make them smile?*** I let this positive intent guide me outwards: I peruse the line of shoppers ahead of me and let my thoughts linger on the assistant diligently bleeping everyone's shopping. Through repetition of the questions, I decide to engage with the assistant – some simple small talk – hoping for a positive moment that could illicit a smile.

Except the queue moves slowly. My time is short. And they look like the chatty type. So when I get to the front of the queue, still happily asking my questions, I step back from verbalising my thoughts and leave the shop without saying a word.

If I link the *outcome* of this process to an external action, to helping others or making them smile, then my immediate reaction in this scenario is *failure.* I haven't reached out. I've remained locked inside my internal thoughts. Already I am switching to negative thoughts about my inability to engage. But is this a failure? *Absolutely not.* I've just spent five minutes *not* being depressed. Thinking *positive* thoughts. Truly *seeing* the world around me. ***This. Is. Success.*** I should leave the shop and punch the air in recognition of my positive thoughts and the transformational change *within* me.

Would it have been different if I *had* spoken to the shop assistant? Yes, I believe it would have been. I might have double-punched the air for taking that additional step. Acting upon the questions is like a virtuous circle. Each outcome you create, however small or inconsequential, will provide genuine pleasure in knowing that it originated entirely from The Kind Mind Method. You, and this thought process, have created *that* moment. Your dopamine hit will flow into the next repetition, and this will encourage you to engage further with the questions. It might be simply starting a conversation, opening a door for a stranger or making a call, but you should celebrate each of these moments because it's these real-world actions that will embed the thought process deeper within you.

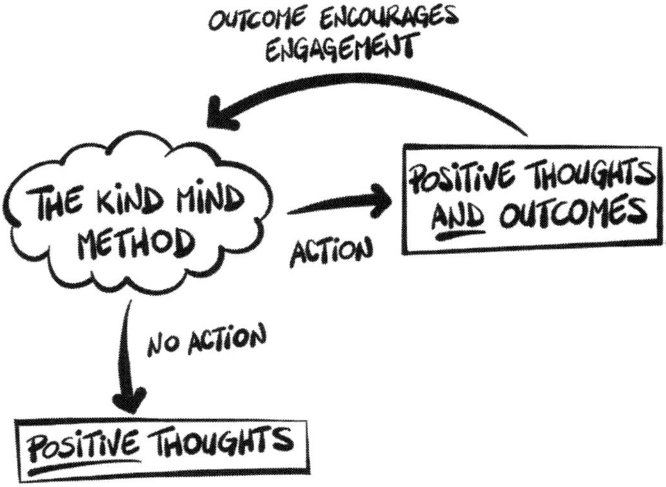

Let's take a brief second example: running. I used to love the solitude and mental space that running gave me, but my depression robbed me of that freedom. It's very different now. When I walk out of my front door, the first thoughts on my mind are typically the two questions: ***How can I help them? How can I make them smile?*** I rarely have *any* idea where these thoughts will take me, but I trust them. I understand that wherever we go, it will be a *good* place. And yes, my thoughts may often drift off into darker and more negative places, but I always have these questions to bring me back to the light.

Thirty minutes later, I may return home with an idea. A thought that emerged from my positive musings, a thought that I can action. A call to a friend. A text message. An email. And I should celebrate every single one. On other days, I may have nothing. There may have been no specific resolution or outcome from my thoughts. *Is this failure?* I've just spent thirty minutes daydreaming. Thinking *good thoughts.* Considering how I can positively engage with the people and the world around me. As before, that shouldn't be considered a failure of this thought process. ***This. Is. Success.***

For this process to provide lasting change, it is essential that you challenge yourself and step out of your mind to act upon your positive thoughts. But always remember: there should be no pressure or burden within you. Doing a good deed is not the *outcome* you are seeking. The true purpose of this book, and these questions, is the shift in your *internal thinking* and the ease with which you are able to switch from negative to positive thoughts. It is all within *you. Your* mind. *Your* thoughts.

4

SCIENCE

A brief look behind the scenes.

QUESTIONS?

The idea of shifting your mental state by having an internal conversation is not a new one. Positive self-talk was used long before the internet turbocharged its acceptance with well-meaning memes promoting aspirational mantras. *I am strong. I am confident. I am successful.* The internet may well tell me that these wishful words can reduce anxiety and stress, but looking back at my previous mental state, I recognise why this never felt right to me. Simply repeating a positive trait I aspired to when I was suffering from depression and negative thoughts would simply have shone a light on my fragile state of mind and reminded me that I *wasn't* strong, confident or successful. They are hollow wishes that offer no practical steps to achieve the aspirational outcomes they promise.

The Kind Mind Method is different – and the science backs that up. Studies have proved that the use of interrogative self-talk (asking yourself a question) consistently drives more positive behaviours and outcomes. In one study[1], a number of volunteers carried out several experiments that used simple tasks (such as solving an anagram or remembering a sequence of numbers) to test this hypothesis. Some of the participants were told to think about *whether* they would complete the tasks (*will I?*), while others were told to think that they *would* complete them (*I will*). In every instance, the participants asking themselves a question performed significantly better. A question demands an answer. It pushes you to think and challenge yourself. In essence, as the study concluded, a question will *"elicit more reasons for action, resulting in goal-directed behaviour"*.

Telling yourself *I will* may provide some brief positive momentum. Asking yourself *will I?* can drive thought and consideration about the task ahead of you. Rather than having simple faith that the positive words will sink into your subconscious, framing the words differently activates the conscious mind and forces you to address the question. Negative thoughts are briefly swept aside as you move into an *active* thinking mode, directly engaging with the wider world and the problem at hand. Take the following positive affirmation examples:

- I am going to smash this presentation!
- I will get this promotion!
- I am calm...

You can repeat each of these hundreds of times and they are unlikely to provide any meaningful guidance on how to achieve the overall objective. Now reframe those words and repeat each of these over and over again:

- How can I smash this presentation?
- How can I get this promotion?
- How can I remain calm?

With both approaches, repeating the words as a mantra can take you briefly away from any negative thoughts. But in the first example, that will be as far as it goes. When the repetition stops, you're left with nothing but an echo of positivity that flutters quickly away. With the latter approach, you're left with *thoughts, ideas, options.* The questions pose a challenge to the mind, a creative springboard to help you mentally engage both internally and externally.

There is no doubt about which will have the better outcome in the long term, but the difficulty with embedding interrogative self-talk into everyday usage is the amount of mental dexterity required to maintain questions that are relevant for a wide range of situations. Stress at work. Problems at home. Health issues.

What questions could possibly support you with this breadth of worry? The limitless boundaries of life make it impossible to conjure up a timely thought that allows you to benefit from this cognitive approach.

The Kind Mind Method is the key to unlocking this powerful capability. The simplicity of the questions provides a constant foundation to rely upon. They are accessible. Easy to remember. And provide an endless and varied opportunity to explore the world around you. Most importantly, whenever you ask the questions, they will *always* draw you into creative, constructive and positive thinking.

KINDNESS

There is one additional – and vital – element that we should not leave out when discussing the power of this process to ward off negative thinking: *kindness.* In 2021, the University of Sussex, in partnership with BBC Radio 4, led 'The Kindness Test', an online questionnaire to learn more about people's attitudes and experiences of kindness and how this might relate to health, wellbeing and other social and psychological experiences[2]. And amongst the plethora of data from over 60,000 responses, what came out was a clear link between wellness and carrying out acts of kindness. This directly correlates with a large body of previous research showing that, very simply, doing good things makes us feel better[3].

These kind acts don't need to be large or burdensome tasks, either. In fact, the data from The Kindness Test identified that the number one way people were kind was simply to *"help people when they ask"*.

But does the *volume* of kind acts make any difference to our overall wellbeing? A 2019 study[4] looked at exactly this by analysing how people felt after performing kind acts for just seven days. These acts of kindness extended to friends and strangers alike, and once again, the resulting data showed a clear increase in happiness within this short window of time. Not only that, there was also a positive correlation between the *number* of kind acts and the overall level of wellbeing. It would indeed seem that the *kinder* you are, the *better* you will feel.

Although there is a sea of data available to provide supporting evidence for the link between kindness and positive mental health, I believe the true power of The Kind Mind Method cannot be found through analysis and research. It is there for all of us to see. A truth that needs no supporting evidence beyond our shared belief. It is the power of good *within* each and every one of us. Belief that there is an intrinsic desire in all of us to do good. To be better. To be *kind.*

Ask yourself: are you a kind person? You may consider your hectic family life. The stress of work. The friend that volunteers at a food bank. Your colleague who runs marathons for charity or looks after an elderly relative. It's so easy for life to get in the way of good intentions, and a comparative view of other people's good deeds can cloud our judgement. For that reason, many people might respond to that question with a disappointed *no.*

But the question hides the internal intent within most of us, so let's reframe it. Do you *want* to be a kind person? *Of course you do.* Who wouldn't *want* to be kind? You may not have the time, energy or mental capacity to translate this positive intent into kind actions, but it still remains within. A singular and motivating force built from the deepest foundation of our personality and how we see our place in the world.

This is the ultimate truth behind The Kind Mind Method.

Whenever I ask the two questions, and it doesn't matter in what context or audience they are aimed at, they always show me a different version of myself. The better person I aspire to be. A *kinder* person. And because of that, I chase the desirable outcome that answering the questions can provide. *How can I help them?* The kindness draws me in, gently placing an embracing arm around my shoulder and inviting me to enter the positive mental space that is now open for me to explore. *How can I make them smile?* This aspirational vision creates a desirable world to immerse myself in and makes stepping away from negativity simple.

The questions open up a better and brighter world, and the intrinsic belief that I am a kind person encourages me to keep asking and answering them.

QUESTION + KINDNESS

This is not a solution born out of research and analysis. It arrived within me like the bewilderment and pleasure of a surprise party. Through time and usage, though, I can now see the powerful influence of kindness in making these questions so special.

They can be used in *any* circumstance without ever becoming repetitive. They drive actions and outcomes that will tangibly change you. They provide a launchpad for creative thoughts and daydreams. In the simplest terms, they *need* to be answered. And the true magic? The fundamental part of the equation that changes everything? The answer is always a positive one. A *kind* one.

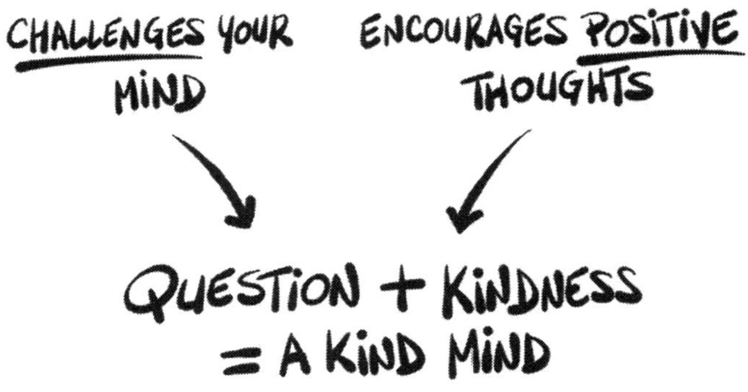

IN THE REAL WORLD: **THE SCHOOL RUN**

"It was while I was doing the school run that I realised the answer to these questions could be as simple as starting a conversation.

It's a ten-minute walk to the school, and before I discovered these questions, our walk would often be in silence or, at best, a conversation squeezed through the fog of my flustered mind. My thoughts were always consumed with the work day ahead, the household admin or irrelevant worries that I could do nothing about while walking my children to school.

On the first day of asking these questions, the school run changed forever.

As my worries took hold, I started asking the questions. Over and over. Then I looked down to my left. The desire to answer the questions with my children as the focal point was like a physical sensation. My worry seemed so inconsequential, and at that precise moment, I knew that I wanted to help them or make them smile more than anything in the universe. It didn't matter how. I just knew at an instinctive level that I needed to make it happen.

So I asked questions. I made some jokes. I talked about our weekend ahead. Listened when they told me about their new Xbox game. There was no specific agenda or thought about how I could help them or make them smile. It was simply the gentle pressure of the questions pushing me outward to engage and talk with the most important people in my life.

These questions have walked with us every day since. Their power to snap me into the moment has remained as strong as the first day I asked them.

I'm sure we would all agree that there are rarely moments where I offer any particular help. But there are always smiles. Lots of them."

5

WHO ARE THEY?

Anyone.
Everyone.

THE TARGET AUDIENCE

How can I help **them**? How can I make **them** smile? Who are the mysterious people that you are asking yourself to interact with and help? Should you always focus on your family and friends, or simply the person nearest to you? Who is behind the generic label of '*them*'?

Realistically, it is anyone and everyone. They can be people you love and share your life with, a stranger you have never met, a voice at the end of the telephone or a friend waiting in the pub. There is no limit. The opportunity to explore '*them*' is endless; the questions can be repeated over and over again with a different audience and a different answer *every* time.

There is real benefit in having this scope to explore, but it is important to have some structure in your thinking. Within this section, we'll cover a number of areas that will help guide you through the initial stages of using The Kind Mind Method:

- Active engagement
- Passive engagement
- Social anxiety
- Find an anchor

- Strangers
- Positive intent

ACTIVE ENGAGEMENT

Active engagement represents the moments you use the questions in the *presence* of other people while making them the focal point. Using the questions in this way is a hugely powerful tool for bringing you into the moment. Nothing snaps you away from your internal thoughts as quickly or effectively as asking these questions and having an audience around you to direct your thoughts onto.

The immediate presence of others provides a tangible reference point for the questions. Someone you can touch and feel rather than simply visualise. Instead of '*them*', it becomes Andy, Laura, Stuart or Kim. And each time, you will be forced to look beyond the internal world and truly consider these people like never before. Their presence demands positive attention – regardless of whether you are with friends, family or a total stranger.

In the past, one of the biggest worries I had was the feeling that there was nothing I could add to a conversation. This drove much of my social anxiety, and there was an unfortunate reality to the fear. So much of my mental energy was exerted on my internal world, a world I could never share beyond the boundary of my own mind, that I did indeed have less to say. I would rely on platitudes, questions or alcohol to deflect attention from myself or bolster my output. At events, I would often feel disassociated from crowds, the people around me blurring out of focus as my thoughts moved inward, making it harder and harder to engage. I could be holding a conversation while an internal monologue berated me for being so boring.

Using The Kind Mind Method harnesses this power for good, enabling you to have parallel thoughts while you socialise. As you talk to others, the questions form a background chatter that forces you to look outwards and challenge yourself to engage. ***How can I help them? How can I make them smile?*** At a party, a crowd is no longer something to fear. It becomes an opportunity: so many people you can help, so many you can make smile. Your positive thoughts can be cast across the room: so many targets, so many possibilities. And all the while you are doing this, your negative thoughts are being crushed. There's no room for anxiety and doubt if internally you keep repeating the questions and focussing on the people around you.

I have no doubt that a big contributor to the evolution of this process was the fact I made the discovery while I was away with friends for a weekend. It was a huge source of anxiety before we arrived. But once I'd discovered the questions, I was immersed with opportunities. Every waking moment, I was with other people: friends and strangers alike. For every mental gap, where in the past I would have filled my mind with negativity, I used this process. I asked questions. I opened doors. I washed dishes. I poured wine. I made food. I talked. I *really* talked. All through the lens of those two questions, constantly pushing me outwards while simultaneously shrinking my fear to nothing.

PASSIVE ENGAGEMENT

Passive engagement represents the time you are using The Kind Mind Method on your own and visualising your engagement with others. These will generally be moments of solitude, time when you have no other external focal point and only your thoughts to keep you company. Where negative thinking may have once prospered, now you have a world of opportunities to explore. Everyone is available for you to consider how you could help them or make them smile.

Passive engagement doesn't provide the same immediate sense of bringing you into the moment as active engagement: you don't have a real person standing before you allowing you to target the questions at them. But it does provide more scope and opportunity to roam free. In fact, you have an entire world to explore within the confines of your mind.

PASSIVE ENGAGEMENT

As someone who is prone to daydream, I find that passive engagement provides a safe place to explore my thoughts, and I usually apply a liberal interpretation to the questions and audience when I'm thinking in passive mode. So many seemingly inconsequential decisions and actions have come from these moments. A family Zoom call. An amusing text to my friends. A question to my wife. A gift for my sons. In isolation, tiny moments that often go unnoticed by the recipient.

For me, though, they are utterly transformative. I see the genesis of every one of these actions clearly, and they provide ongoing confirmation of the positive shift I have made in my behaviour, moving my focus from the inner me to absolutely anyone and everyone I know.

SOCIAL ANXIETY

We previously explored how powerful the questions can be when used in the presence of other people (active engagement), but that's not the only way they can help in social situations. Think for a moment of a future social or work situation that could cause you some anxiety. Maybe it's a meeting, a networking event or simply drinks with friends. The situation is irrelevant, the constant is the low-level anxiety that the thought of it brings *beforehand*. You'll be reluctant to cast your mind to that future as it will only serve to increase your levels of anxiety. Not when you use The Kind Mind Method.

Instead of turning away from the event, simply repeat the two questions and shift your attention directly into it and, more specifically, the people that will be there. ***How can I help them? How can I make them smile?*** You are no longer looking at the event with fear, you are problem-solving, thinking of ways you can engage, stories you can tell. These passive thoughts may just float lazily through your mind, but when you are at the event and engaging actively with the people around you, it will be these floating thoughts that you will be able to quickly reach for and deploy.

There is a second element that can help with social events: *charging yourself up*. This is all about confidence. It is best done as close as possible to the event – walking to the pub or waiting anxiously for your meeting to start. This is about repeatedly shouting the words in your mind. It's about bouncing on your toes with excitement while the words echo through your mind. It's about drowning out negativity and anxiety with a crashing wave of positivity that you can surf into the situation on. ***How can I help them? How can I make them smile?*** Over and over you repeat the words, cycling through the people that you'll be seeing in just a few moments, all the while shouting the questions internally. You'll enter the situation in a positive, inquisitive and relaxed manner. Ready to engage rather than retreat.

FIND AN ANCHOR

If your thoughts are anything like mine, they can often be chaotic and frustratingly difficult to grasp hold of. They talk over each other, they appear from nowhere, shout in your face, then run into the woods to draw you into the darkness with a mental game of hide and seek. So, while you're trying your best to manage them through the use of this process, it helps to have a constant point of reference you can draw upon as thoughts tumble randomly around your head. For me, it's my family.

At times when I find my thoughts running free, and I reach for the questions to help bring me back into the moment, I have a default – and critically, *easy* – point of reference that I can focus on. My wife. My children. ***How can I help them? How can I make them smile?*** They are an ever-present, a happy place. I know that if I can successfully answer the questions, it will bring benefit to the family. I don't need to be in their presence; I see them so clearly, whether they're sitting next to me on the sofa or they're hundreds of miles away. They are always with me and provide the simplest of anchors that I can always turn to. There is no effort to focus. They are just there.

Your anchor doesn't need to be your family, but it should be an individual (or group of people) that you can easily visualise. My family are not *always* the people I think of when repeating the questions, but they are the *easiest* to picture. It's a slight but important distinction. When I'm tired or alone and have little energy to extend my thinking, I can repeat the questions and simply let the most important people in my life float through my mind.

STRANGERS

This has truly been one of the most revelatory aspects of this journey. I have always considered talking to strangers for no reason whatsoever slightly weird. Actually, a *lot* weird. I don't mean engaging with a shopkeeper or any of the other millions of trivial reasons you may exchange a pleasantry with a random stranger, I mean actually striking up a conversation with someone you don't know or have never met. Literally, just turning to them, maybe on a bus or standing in a queue. A total stranger. And then start talking. For no reason. I just don't get it. Or I should say, I didn't. Until I started using The Kind Mind Method.

When you turn to the questions for support, either through active or passive engagement, your focus will generally be on people from within your social circle. Switching that focus to a person, or group of people, within your proximity *that you do not know* has the potential to drive a tangible change in your behaviour. Not only that, but it will also bring you into the moment, the absolute here and now, better than any other mental mind trick you may have tried.

This is an extension of active engagement, focussing not just on people you know, but on anyone and everyone around you, regardless of the relationship you may (or may not) have with them. Because you have no prior knowledge of the person you are focussing on, it makes the question much more complex and provides a fundamentally different engagement. You really need to think about the questions. ***How can I help them? How can I make them smile?*** If you don't know them, then it can be a huge challenge. What would make them smile? How do you know if you can help them? How can you say anything without coming across as a bit strange? It's this challenge that means you have to work at the question, think about it, consider the options and situation. But when you do engage and interact, the sense of success is huge.

When I consider engaging in this way, I become hyper-aware of my surroundings, the people, their actions and the possibilities it may provide. The challenge takes me entirely away from any internal thoughts and back into the moment. As I repeat the words over and over, it gives me the confidence to act in ways I never would have thought possible. I *do* now speak to strangers. Not all the time, and rarely beyond a few positive words or a small gesture: asking the supermarket shop assistant how their day is going, a smile shared as I queue in the café, a breathless exchange at the gym. Most importantly, and significantly different from 'before', I am *aware* of the people around me. No longer are they simply the unseen audience to the theatre of my mind.

There is always a significant sense of achievement when I do reach out and engage with a stranger. I have done *something,* a tangible action to make their day better. An action I would *never* have contemplated with my previous state of mind and a genuine shift in my outward behaviour. I celebrate every one of these actions, knowing that they only exist due to the use of these simple questions.

POSITIVE INTENT

How I use The Kind Mind Method has evolved over the years. Initially, I would always try to actively engage with the questions, and I believe this was the mental shove I needed to send me out into the wider world and away from negative thinking. As time passed and the triggers and anxiety reduced, I often found that I wasn't engaging directly with the questions to the same level. I was still using them to drive my engagement with others and filling my quiet moments with proactive usage. Sometimes, though, when I found a negative thought creeping in through the backdoor of my mind, I would simply repeat the words a couple of times and that would be enough to bring me into the moment and shift my thinking away to something different. I didn't need to engage with the questions; the mere act of repeating them was enough to snap my thoughts away from negativity.

I believe this is due to the internal weight of the words. However sceptical you may be about this approach, I can assure you that every word about my mental state – and the transformative power and speed of this thought process in changing it – *is true*. On the Friday before my weekend away in the Yorkshire Dales,

I worried about *everything.* I woke up on the Monday, bleary-eyed and confused at the profound freedom of thoughts I suddenly had.

These words are more than just words to me. They saved me, and I truly believe they continue to do so on a daily basis. They constantly push me to be a better person. They are my safe, positive place, and it is this sensation that I draw upon whenever I repeat them. Even when I don't engage with the questions directly, I relax into the words and let them flow through me. I see them clearly and hear them loudly, but sometimes I will only draw upon the *positive intent.* There is no specific person that I am focussing on to help or illicit a smile from. If anything, my thoughts will linger on myself, and I'll celebrate the control that the questions have provided and enjoy the positive sensation of the words.

In many respects, I am using the questions much more like a traditional mantra on these occasions. They are inspiring words that provide a focal point and an underlying sense of wellbeing. This isn't something I would recommend from the outset. This sense of positivity can only be generated from confidence. It offers me this calm because I *know* it works. If you simply started on day one repeating the words with no focal point, engagement or action, the words would carry no weight. Be patient, and when you have seen the true benefit of the words, then you will be able to use them with *positive intent.*

IN THE REAL WORLD: **DOWNWARD DOG**

"The quiet of my yoga class would provide a wealth of opportunities to use The Kind Method. One evening I decided to keep my focus in the room, considering the strangers around me. There seemed to be little opportunity for wider engagement as everyone was intently focussed on their personal journey of stretching and straining.

I was relaxed about this. My outlook was that my time thinking positive thoughts, of any description, was better than worry or fear. So, I continued. If I caught myself drifting into a negative thought, I would come back to the questions and the people around me.

It was about five minutes before the end that our instructor, Anthony, whilst contorting in a way that no septuagenarian should ever be able to, prompted us to shift onto our left foot and inhale deeply into the stretch. And here it was, my opportunity. I sensed some confusion in the room, a pause before moving, and a couple of heads glanced upwards, but my senses were primed to engage. I'd been searching for ways to help my classmates. My words leapt out.

'Err, Anthony, we've already done the left side, we're onto the right now.'

A confused look. A shake of the head. An apology, and off we went on the right foot.

A monumentally small moment in someone's day. An utterly inconsequential comment that probably could have gone unspoken with little or no impact on the remainder of the class. Not for me. In my mind, it was cause for celebration. I'd been constantly looking to engage in impossible circumstances with a room full of middle-aged people that I had never once uttered a word to. I bounced out of that yoga class knowing that however small and irrelevant it may have been, I had helped them in the end."

SUMMARY

- Use the questions when you are with friends, family and colleagues to relentlessly drive your thoughts outwards and into the *moment.*
- When you are alone, enjoy the safe space these thoughts provide by *exploring anyone and everyone* to discover positive actions you can take.
- Find someone *close to you as an anchor*: a familiar thought you can draw upon under any circumstances.
- Ask the questions in the *company of strangers* to create transformational change within you.
- When you know this process works, relax into the questions and just *enjoy the calm* that they bring within you.

A BRIEF INTERLUDE

To show you how powerful these questions truly can be.

THE PRESENTATION

When I was depressed, I would typically have hundreds of negative thoughts floating through my mind on a daily basis. I would diligently review them all, skipping nervously past some and dwelling on others. Every now and again, there would be something special. A mental feast that I knew my mind would fixate upon for days or weeks. A thought so powerful and compelling that it would wipe out *everything* else.

There was never any logic or commonality to these titanic worries – except their power to hold me prisoner. When they drifted into my mind, the wider world would drop entirely from my awareness, and I would furiously search for some meaning or solution to the impossible question I was asking. I believe many of you reading this book will know *exactly* what I am talking about. And the question you may be asking is whether this thought process can reach beyond the everyday worries and deal with these all-conquering leviathans of the mind. The answer is yes. *Easily.* Let me rewind to a regular Thursday at work to provide a brief example of how.

It happened in a team meeting. It was the first team meeting I'd held after being promoted to a management position. Although I was previously at a senior level, I'd always been classed as an independent contributor, which essentially meant I'd led people in delivering specific projects and outcomes but never had the formal responsibility of line management and all the extra duties that came with it. But following my promotion, I went from zero to twenty-five people overnight. A daunting figure that, within days, brought me a flurry of nerves. The change had come about as part of a wider organisational reshuffle. Anyone working within a corporate environment will know that every few years there will generally be some level of change – sometimes a minor shuffle of functions, other times it's like throwing a pack of cards in the air: everyone ends up somewhere different and you usually lose a couple. This was the fifty-two-card pick-up version.

Following the change, there was chaos. Different interpretations of the new ways of working danced across the teams, and process changes evolved like Chinese whispers as people tried to adapt, with no real clue of what they should be doing and how. Everyone had their own agenda and priorities. While this was going on, I had twenty-five people who'd been shifted from various parts of the business and landed into my team. Some of them knew me, while to others I was just the guy who used to be in pre-sales and looked about seventeen.

As we progressed through the initial stages of the change, I was keen to provide assurance and stability to my new team. I wanted to give them confidence they had a leader with vision, and a role with purpose. I scheduled an initial session with the team to introduce myself, an opportunity to set out my stall as both their manager and a person. We were all working remotely from home, so I was keen to provide some insight about myself, not just about my professional background, but personal details that would help build relationships and smooth the transition.

So here we were, a video conference call with my new team and a single slide to talk through and introduce myself. A slide about *me*, personal and professional, and a subject I should know better than anyone. It was carefully crafted, a timeline of my experience to subliminally assure them they were in safe hands: photos of me, my family, my hobbies and from the aftermath of the catastrophic accident ten years earlier that had left me with a broken neck. Finally, I added a picture of Doogie Howser that would be my comedy finale (and provide the additional benefit of allowing me to drop my *actual* age into the meeting so they wouldn't continue to think I was seventeen).

Good presentations are all about crafting a story: make it interesting, take the audience on a journey and have a point you want to get across. Drafting and delivering presentations had always been one of my strengths. As much as I could be crippled with self-doubt and worry on almost any subject, I knew that when I was on stage or at the front of a room with PowerPoint at my side, *I was good.* I could read the room. I would project my voice and engage. I would tell a story and people would listen.

I was also, always, nervous. It was constantly there, ready to reach out from the side of the stage like a long shepherd's crook and yank me breathlessly to the side. On several occasions over the years, the nerves had materialised during a presentation, always at the start and always sucking the breath from my body, causing my words to quiver and my mind to freeze. I had mechanisms to deal with it; usually, running through the material beforehand would be enough to ensure everything went as it should. It had been at least ten years since I'd suffered any problems.

Back, then, to my team meeting. A quick thirty-minute intro about me and my vision for the team; my first real opportunity to steady the ship and outline the direction of travel. There was no need to run through the slide in advance; the flow was clear in my mind. Anyway, I was going to be talking about *me.* Surely that's one topic I should know better than anyone? I hadn't really accounted for the crushing volume of meetings and calls that were coming at me from all angles. I flew from meeting to meeting with rarely a break and never moving from my seat, so it was an apologetic and distracted me that landed three minutes late onto the team call. *And then it happened.*

The initial part of the meeting was fine, and there was some general discussion as we settled into the call. The problem only started when I began to share my screen and present my slides. The moment the slide flicked on, my mind froze. I was sitting in my office, at home, with no one else in the room. I had a small speaker/microphone in front of me, and the weight of expectation suddenly struck me as the enormity of *everything* I was taking on flooded through me and squeezed the air from my lungs: *I am managing twenty-five people; I have to prioritise what we are going to transform for the next three years; I have four more meetings today on completely different topics I don't understand; I have to support the business case for the financial approval or everything collapses around me.* All this and more. It began to crush me like the depths of the sea. My words started to come out but they were breathless and barely coherent. My voice quivered and I repeatedly gasped for breath. A shocked silence blared from my microphone as the gaping jaws of confusion I was imagining from the audience snaked out and curled round my throat to further restrict my breathing and my thoughts. I sputtered on for about ten minutes, possibly the longest ten minutes of my life, before I was finally rescued with a question.

'So how did you break your neck?' asked one of the team.

I was suddenly glad I had decided to include this in my slides, and it was probably the first time I had been grateful for the accident that had shaped so much of the past decade. The question broke the spell and cleared my mind. I was able to pause, take a breath and respond to a simple question rather than have the weight of presenting pull me down. I answered the question and felt the confidence build; I ran through the last fifteen minutes as normal. The damage was done, though. It was, without any doubt whatsoever, an absolute fucking disaster.

In these types of scenarios, people often tell you that *maybe it wasn't that bad,* or *I'm sure you thought it was worse than everyone else.* I don't find this helpful. I was there, and I know how bad it was. It was *very* bad. I was in a quivering, breathless, nervous state, and that was just while presenting a slide. A slide about *me.* Surely this wasn't the leadership they wanted to guide them through the choppy waters of a huge organisational restructuring? The person they would want to represent their deliverables up the chain to management? Especially someone who can't even present a slide about himself?

My immediate response after the meeting was curiosity. For the past few months, I'd been entirely free from depression and anxiety through the use of The Kind Mind Method. I'd assumed it would provide protection from all situations, and this anomaly had raised some doubts in my mind. So I made a decision. I would let the thought in. I would let the *worry* in. I would look back at the meeting and just let my mind wander free to see whether there was some hidden truth I could discover about the situation. I vividly recall the moment. I was in the car park at Asda and about to do the weekly shop. I stepped out and left the protection of my two questions in the car. For the first time in several months, I would stop asking them and simply see where my thoughts took me.

When I let my mind roam free, I was immediately transported back to the meeting. I began to relive my breathless and idiotic mumbling in Ultra HD. A new and terrible reality was emerging from my mind as I forensically examined the meeting. My creative mind was filling in the mental gaps. I imagined the gaping expressions of my team members, the whispers of incredulity and the disparaging messages they were surely typing as I fumbled on with my presentation.

A rapid-fire procession of *what if?* scenarios queued for my attention. What if my boss hears about this? What if everyone leaves my team? What if they tell everyone else how useless I am? The tickle of imposter syndrome that had distracted me over the past few weeks had suddenly solidified into a tangible reality. *It only took an hour.* A single hour absorbed in the awful memory of the past.

When I returned to my car with six heavy bags of shopping, I was unsure if I would be able to turn up for work the next day. The impact of my actions at the meeting felt utterly catastrophic. Irreversible actions that would cement people's opinion of me forever. I felt lost. Scared. Despondent at what had happened and the terrible outcomes still to come. I put my head in my hands and sobbed.

And then I stopped and made a simple decision. Once more I began to ask myself those two simple questions. *Over and over.*

Within minutes my thinking had shifted away from the negative tragedy I had created. Not only had it shifted, but I was able to focus back into the issue and look for a positive way to engage. ***How can I help them? How can I make them smile?*** I focussed on my team members. I considered positive actions I could take. I planned meetings. I plotted our team vision, the team goals. I completely discarded the negative thinking, and through those simple questions, I steamrolled forward with actions and outcomes.

The negative memory was an alluring and powerful one. But each time it reached out to me, I would contrast it with the positive aspirations of the questions. I would *see* the two options: one, a negative and imaginary world of despair, the second, a world of possibility that I could achieve through my positive thinking and actions. *I always made the right choice.*

Without the protection of this thought process, I truly don't know if I would have had the courage to continue in my role. The fictional world I had created in just one hour was so powerful, so dreadful, that I believe it could have utterly shattered my confidence and warped my future. *None of this happened.* All because I continually and relentlessly asked myself two simple questions. Two questions that gave me an option. A *better* world to dream of.

These questions may seem simple to you. They may even seem a bit trivial. But I truly believe they are the most powerful words I have ever spoken. The most powerful words I continue to speak. Every single day.

6

CONTEXT IS KING

Learning how and when to ask these questions.

CONTEXT

How and when you deploy this process is just as important as the content of the words. They act in different ways depending on the *circumstances* you use them in and drive different outcomes based upon your intent. To break this down, we must look in more detail at the different *contexts* they can be used in.

The **reactive context** is when you ask the questions to *react* to an internal state of mind. This will typically be either negative thoughts or an emotional response such as anger or anxiety. The key principle is that you are not reacting to the trigger that may have caused your worry. Internal and external triggers are, in some cases, out of your control. Your response will be to the mental situation that you are subsequently building.

The **proactive context** is when you use this process to fill the *gaps* in your thinking. You are starting with no negative thoughts or emotions to manage; instead, you are providing your creative mind with a universe of positive opportunities to explore.

They will always remain the same words that you repeat in each situation. But the underlying impact will vary greatly depending on the *context.*

REACTIVE CONTEXT: MANAGING NEGATIVE THOUGHTS

One of the most critical elements of this process is the ability it will provide you to seamlessly step away from simple worries or powerful negative thoughts. It's not about *stopping* negative thoughts. Far from it. Instead, the questions provide the relevant knowledge you need to make an informed decision about where to focus your mental time and energy. They do this by:

- Helping you to **SEE** your negative thoughts.
- Providing you with a **CHOICE** of thoughts to engage with.
- Indulging your **CREATIVITY** to ensure you don't return to more negative thoughts.

To see how this functions, let's drop briefly into the quantum levels of decision making that occur when I ask these questions in response to a negative thought.

HELPING ME TO SEE A NEGATIVE THOUGHT

Let's imagine a scenario. A typical day. A typical worry. A thought has invaded my mind and decided to claim squatters' rights to my mental capacity. It starts to become *sticky*. It is alluring and I am drawn inwards. I am building a new and twisted reality.

But then...

Firstly, my triggers still exist. They may be fewer and further apart, but they remain, and I suspect they always will. So, I have little or no control over that *initial* spark of fear that may have started everything. But the moment I see the subsequent negative thoughts building in my mind, it is here that I need to deploy the process in the *reactive* context. I am responding, not to the initial trigger, but instead to the internal world of despair I am actively creating. *The worry.* The negative thoughts. At this moment, as I wake and orient my mind, I repeat the words that are so familiar. Words that flow and immediately provide a reassuring arm round my shoulder. ***How can I help them? How can I make them smile?*** I may say the words once. I may repeat them over and over again. Twenty, thirty, forty times or more.

I now have two thoughts competing for my attention. One is a powerful negative thought. A worry. The other is a world of possibility. A bright, bold and constructive thought that can only lead to a positive outcome. ***How can I help them? How can I make them smile?*** I can truly see the two thoughts. Side by side I understand the true nature of each of them. One positive. One negative.

1. THE QUESTIONS HAVE HELPED ME IDENTIFY MY THOUGHT AS BEING NEGATIVE.

Negative thoughts are not easily recognised. They are not labelled for immediate categorisation and mental filing into a suitable location. In the past I could easily spend hours worrying about where the cat was or whether my sore finger would escalate into terminal finger cancer. And the entire time, I would justify it as *planning* or *problem solving*. I would desperately pursue the thought, searching for a solution to the impossible problem I had created in my mind. But there would never be any outcome beyond the time lost in my own thoughts, and I just didn't have the cognitive ability to step back and see that truth.

Do not underestimate the importance of this simple first step. It is only when you understand the true nature of your negative thoughts that you can step away from them.

GIVING ME A CHOICE OF THOUGHTS TO ENGAGE WITH

As I continue to repeat the questions, I start to engage directly with them. Even though the original negative thought is still looming over me, my thoughts are beginning to crystalise into some tangible ideas. What I now have is the second and most crucial element. Something

I had lost as my depression took hold. *A choice.* A true and honest decision about whether to pursue the negative thought or engage my thinking elsewhere – on something better. Something positive.

In the past, I *never* felt like I had this choice. My thoughts would race away from me, diverting in different and completely random directions. I tried *everything.* Nothing worked. Consciously, yes, I was in control of my actions and motor skills. But mentally, I had as much control as a frog strapped to a firework holding on for dear life while hurtling through the air and waiting for the big bang.

It's different now. The questions provide a positive version of me that I aspire to. I *want* to help people; I *want* to make them smile. When we compare this aspirational outcome to the grey and desperate world of fear within my negative thoughts, the stark difference is clear. I can vividly see the two choices: it's like choosing between my old black-and-white TV that I had in my bedroom when I was growing up and the 65-inch Ultra HD TV that entices me with an explosion of colour in the John Lewis showroom. I can choose to stay with my black-and-white world, and it's important that I have that choice to make, but why on earth would I? As I repeat the words and make my decision, I come away from my negative thinking with a safe place to explore. ***How can I help them? How can I make them smile?*** A world of possibility and options. A positive and colourful world of potential.

2. THE THOUGHT PROCESS HAS PROVIDED ME WITH A BETTER OPTION THAT MAKES IT EASIER TO STOP ENGAGING WITH NEGATIVE THINKING.

I HAVE A FOCAL POINT FOR MY CREATIVITY

Now that I have made my decision, I am free to explore my thoughts. ***How can I help them? How can I make them smile?*** When I actively engage with the questions, my mind will move into a completely different way of thinking. I am problem solving. I hear every word and my thoughts turn to actions. I float through my circle of friends, family and colleagues to consider the wide range of ways in which I can help them or make them smile.

I am still daydreaming and liable to be sucked into a mental vortex where time vanishes. The critical difference is that my thoughts are no longer negative. I have chosen a different and more creative path, one that can provide some constructive output to the world rather than pushing me deeper inside my own body and mind.

3. THE QUESTIONS GIVE ME A CONSTRUCTIVE THOUGHT TO FOCUS MY MENTAL ENERGY ON.

REACTIVE CONTEXT: MANAGING YOUR EMOTIONS

In the previous section we broke down how these questions help you to respond to, and manage, negative thoughts. Staying within the reactive context, the other area to examine is *emotional* responses.

In the past, my negative thinking could consume my mind for hours. I would search for a worry, create an internal world around it and then seamlessly insert my future or past self into the leading role. These thoughts were always vivid. Rich, powerful and dense narratives that could run for days, weeks or months.

It is different with emotional responses such as anger, annoyance, fear and anxiety. They can be just as negative or destructive, but typically there are no tangible thoughts to hold onto. Emotions prioritise *feelings* over thoughts. The *flutter* of fear. The *heat* of anger. The *quivering* voice of anxiety. But with this process, we can respond to our feelings just as we did with negative thoughts. To provide an example, let's go back to the days *before* I discovered The Kind Mind Method.

I'm running through the park, the sun shining on a crisp Spring morning as the dew sparkles on the grass around me. It's early and people are scattered across the park: jogging, walking, talking, and breathing in the fresh smell of possibility that lingers in the air. I'm unaware of most of this as my thoughts are all inward and negative. So I plod on, oblivious of the sun, or Spring or sparkly grass. Essentially, I am retaining a peripheral awareness of my surroundings that is just about enough to stop me from falling over my own feet and not much more.

As I stumble around a corner, I come across an elderly couple walking their small dog. They don't see me, the dog scampers across my path, and in my distracted state, I only just manage to dodge past it by pivoting towards them. Still carrying my forward momentum, and with the shock of being catapulted from my internal thoughts to navigating a geriatric assault course while being chased by a Sausage dog, I try to move sideways to avoid them. The couple comically mirror my movements, at a significantly age-reduced level, and we do a brief and awkward dance before I finally manage to navigate my way past the dog, the lead and the pensioners. We both manage an apologetic wave and then move on.

Well, maybe *they* do. I'd just spent the previous twenty minutes in an entirely imaginary and negative world within the confines of my mind, and the catastrophic scenario I'd been building had been brutally interrupted by the dithering couple. What were they doing just standing in the middle of the path? Don't they realise what I'm dealing with? OK, maybe they're not mind readers, and actually, all of my worry is entirely ridiculous and imaginary, but surely, at the very least they should have been able to keep their attack (Sausage) dog on a lead!

I may have thrown them a polite smile as I jogged past, but inside I am apoplectic. My constructed world of fear is melting away with fury and starting to crystallise into a new thought that I'm ashamed to admit does indeed involve a significant amount of grievous bodily harm to a senior citizen or two.

The anger is utterly irrational. Fuelled by my negative thinking, it flashes brightly, sending triggers spreading through my body. It's a simple and perpetual loop. My initial negative thoughts now feed the overreaction and drive me further inward, with even more damaging thoughts to pursue.

Using the questions to stop this, or any other emotive overreaction, is simple. Firstly, you are not going to respond to the external stimulus of the pensioners and their Sausage dog. That is an external trigger out of your control. It has happened. You can't change that. Instead, you are going to respond to the emotion you have internally generated. The irrational anger. The overreaction. As it builds and consumes you, as you become aware of the sensations within your body, you simply repeat the words. ***How can I help them? How can I make them smile?***

Over and over again, take yourself away from the emotion and move your thinking back to a rational and pragmatic place. In many respects, this initial response can be the equivalent of a mental timeout. A blanket to smother the oxygen that fuels the fire of anger. A deep breath or ten-count to let your anger subside. Repeat it again. And again. And again. You don't even need to hear the words. It is a familiar and safe place that simply gives you time. ***How can I help them? How can I make them smile?*** And space. ***How can I help them? How can I make them smile?***

The words act in subtle and different ways. They stop the emotion, a short, sharp slap in the face that brings you back into the moment and helps you to see the situation for what it is. The positive intent of the words provides you with a better option. As you repeat them over and over again, you can decide to engage directly with the questions and move completely away from both negative thinking and the emotional response you've been having. You always have the option to indulge your anger, but in these situations, I have found that the positive intent and mental breathing space the questions provide will ensure I make the right choice.

Although this approach works for all emotional responses (anger, frustration, embarrassment, annoyance, to name but a few), the initial action is primarily about allowing you to pause and step away from your immediate (and potentially irrational) reaction. It allows you to shift your thinking to a more positive place. In time, when you reflect on these moments, you will often not be able to find the source of anger or frustration; it will simply be erased through time and momentum.

In other cases, though, you may feel there is a more genuine reason for your response, a true justification for being annoyed or angry, rather than a ludicrous response to a stray Dachshund. This is entirely valid.

In these situations, I still urge you to use this process. No argument is best had when angry; no annoyance will fade while you fuel it. Ask the questions. Shift your thinking elsewhere and come back to it at a later point when your thoughts are more considered and rational. However, there is a difference in this situation that should be noted.

Where there is a specific person who is the source of your frustration, and there is a genuine reason for your response, then it is best not to engage the questions with them as the focal point. *Shift your focus outside the point of frustration and onto others: friends, family, colleagues or strangers.* It doesn't matter who it is; the critical aspect is that you move your focus elsewhere, into a positive engagement beyond the boundaries of the emotion. If you immediately pivot to the source of frustration and ask these questions with that individual in mind, it will be extremely difficult to move away. There will be an internal conflict between the desire to help and the frustration or annoyance that you were feeling. This conflict will ultimately keep hold of you.

So next time you are arguing with your wife, husband or partner, righteous frustration surging through your body at the words they have spoken, take a step back. Ask yourself. ***How can I help them? How can I make them smile?*** Then immediately think of someone else. Someone distant. Someone different. Rest assured, when you revisit the situation with a calmer mind, there will be a significantly better outcome.

PROACTIVE CONTEXT

In the previous section we talked about using The Kind Mind Method to respond to internal or external triggers and how it provides a more constructive option to negative thinking. In and of itself, this is a huge change, a reality that anyone who struggles with negativity dreams about. It does not stop there, though. Using this process in the *proactive* context takes you beyond simply controlling your thoughts; it actively pushes you outward. It seamlessly guides you to behaviours and actions you *never* would have thought possible. Starting a conversation with a stranger? This will be the highlight of your day, not the incomprehensible action of others. Meeting a large group of colleagues? You can open the conversation without anxiety and fear.

Whereas we used the process in the reactive context to respond to an internal or external trigger, the proactive context needs no prompting. This is all about pre-empting the negative thoughts. Filling your mind with constructive and positive thinking *before negativity has any chance to emerge.* And it's so simple.

In those quiet seconds, the miniscule moments of the day when you are not engaging in negative thoughts, simply start repeating the questions. ***How can I help them? How can I make them smile?*** Brushing your teeth? Ask the questions. On the toilet? Ask the questions. Feeding the cats? Ask the questions. Hoovering? Ask the questions. You get the idea. The key distinction from the reactive context is that you fill your mind with the questions *before* you have started any negative thinking. Any time of the day, any moment where you find yourself briefly free of thoughts (negative or positive), then use the process.

Why do this? Firstly, this stops negative thinking before it has a chance to take hold. By asking yourself those questions, you open up an endless world of positive possibilities to think about. Your thoughts can drift to absolutely anyone your imagination allows, or alternatively, reach out into the physical world around you, to the people near you. The questions can be so broadly interpreted that they are easily applicable to any problem or situation you may be facing. They allow you to reposition a worry into a constructive thought, then into an action and ultimately into a tangible and positive outcome.

The second reason for using the proactive context? *It can, and will, change you.* Not just at an internal level: it directly influences your actions, the things you do and the words you speak. This has been one of the most fundamental and surprising changes brought about by this process.

Proactively thinking provides you with more freedom to engage deeply with the questions. You're not starting with a clutter of negative thoughts to wade through, and it becomes easier to truly consider what you can tangibly do to help someone or to make them smile. This constant repetition, the questions coming over and over again, provides confidence and encouragement to take that next step. To turn a thought into an action. Not just an action, a positive one, *something that adds to the world.* You are contributing, helping, you are doing good. Improving the lives of others.

I can specifically see the benefit of using the process in the proactive context every single Sunday as I take the two-minute walk to the local shop to buy a newspaper. During the time I was depressed, this would have been a slow lumber, where my mind would drift through a kaleidoscope of negative thoughts before grabbing my paper and engaging in the least amount of social interaction possible to conduct the financial transaction. I wasn't purposefully trying to be rude to the person behind the counter; I simply had my head so crammed full of worry that it was difficult to pull myself into the moment and have even the simplest of conversations. If I was asked a question, I would certainly respond, but there was zero chance of me starting a conversation.

My Sunday-morning walk is vastly different now. From the first step I take, I begin to ask the questions in the proactive context. ***How can I help them? How can I make them smile?*** I don't give negative thoughts *any* opportunity to start; my mind is immediately consumed with only positive thinking. Typically, I let my focus drift onto the person behind the counter in the shop, primarily because it is a simple and consistent focal point that I can visualise through the fog of my Sunday-morning mind. I may not know exactly who will be behind the counter, but the pixelated view doesn't stop my constructive thoughts. Is there some comment about the weather I could make that might get a smile? Maybe I could draw attention to my lunatic hair that's protruding so far sideways I can see it in my peripheral vision like a microphone accidentally bobbing into a movie shot.

When I enter the shop, I am filled with positivity and enthusiasm. The unsuspecting shop attendant has absolutely no idea that I have just spent the last two minutes repeatedly considering ways that I can make them smile or help them. Generally speaking, it's quite hard to engage beyond pleasantries, but that's enough. It's more than before. It's a tangible change in my behaviour and the way I engage with others.

At the very least, even on my worst days – with a hangover, my PJs under my clothes and crazy hair protruding in all directions – I always manage a quick 'hello' and 'how are you?' This weekly slice of time is really important and a great example of why the thought process works so well. Before, it was dead time. A brief space that I would always fill with a worry or fear.

Now, even if I don't follow through on my good thoughts and speak to the shop attendant, it's still a huge change. I am *not* being depressed. In fact, more than that, I am not only NOT being depressed, I am actually thinking and doing something positive. I have been thinking *good* thoughts. Even if it's just a two-minute walk to the shop thinking about how I can help a random stranger, it's been two minutes well spent, *whatever* the outcome. This micro-moment is a tangible change from my former self, and if you are able to do this and take the thought process into the many quiet moments of your day, it can be a huge step in shifting you to a more positive frame of mind in everything you do.

IN THE REAL WORLD: **WHATSAPP**

"The idea came to me on the bus. I was staring out of the window and the two questions were occasionally stepping forward to nudge my daydreams away from negative thoughts. The faces of my friends and family floated through my mind as I considered ways I could positively engage with them. I landed on a text to my mum and sister suggesting lunch. But then another thought elbowed itself to the front of my mind. Why on earth don't we have a family WhatsApp chat group?

Five minutes later I had created a group with our entire family in it and texted my Mum with instructions on how Dad could install the app and join the group. We now use it all the time, but I'm the only person that knows the truth about how that group came into existence."

SUMMARY

- At the first hint of a negative thought, ask the questions. They will help you *see* the negative thought. They will give you a *better* thought to choose. They will give you a constructive thought to *immerse* yourself in.
- Respond to emotional triggers by asking the questions. If there is a focal point to your emotion, *shift the questions to someone else.*
- Use The Kind Mind Method proactively by *filling the quiet moments of the day* with the two questions.

7

A DIFFERENT PERSPECTIVE

There's always an option.

YOU CHOOSE

The Kind Mind Method may seem ludicrously simple. Two questions. Repeated. But we have already seen how these questions can be used in different ways: first, to protect you from negative thoughts, and second, to proactively shift your thinking to a more external and positive view of the world. There are many layers within these simple questions, and it goes beyond just the proactive and reactive context we have previously discussed. The intention and variety are essential. The two questions allow a completely different interaction with *any* situation. One element is more social (*smile*) while the other enables a supportive approach (*help*). Combined, they are broad enough to be applied to *any* situation or pinpoint-focussed on a specific problem.

HOW CAN I HELP THEM?

I find there is rarely a simple answer to this question. It isn't a mental 'Q & A' where I throw up a query and dig frantically for a quick solution to fix a problem. It's a repetition over and over, a consideration of my target audience, and from there, further repetition as I consider what *help* could mean within the context of my area of focus:

- I *see* a stranger sitting opposite me on a train. *I repeat the questions.* I really see them. I am aware of them. I consider them and think about ways I could engage with them. I open the door for them when we get off at the same stop.
- While out walking, I visualise my children and consider their schoolwork, their friends and the games they enjoy. *I repeat the questions.* I am exploring them, their lives and interests. Looking for something. Not caring if I find it. Enjoying the time I'm mentally spending with them.
- I *hear* about a work colleague who has been struggling with a presentation. *I repeat the questions.*

> I make a mental note to send them an email offering my support when I'm back at work.

I'm not prescriptive about what the word '*help*' means within this context. This principle applies broadly across both questions; you are not trying to solve a puzzle. There is no pressure or particular outcome associated with the question. If you can engage with someone and help them, that's great. You've helped another person, made their day better in some small way. Maybe you spoke to someone intending to help but ultimately couldn't. That's also great; you've made a connection and engaged socially with someone you wouldn't ordinarily have. And most importantly, when there's no outcome? Remember, you've just spent five minutes thinking positive thoughts about how you can help others – *not* negative thoughts that could have kept you mentally locked inside yourself. *That is success.*

For this process to really work, don't try and overthink or analyse the questions. The most important thing here is that you are brought back into the moment and your thoughts reach outwards to others. Equally, you don't need to use grand gestures or take part in burdensome activities to demonstrate your commitment to making a better you. Simple, small gestures can often mean more in the moment than expensive gifts. Your partner is doing the dishes? Just ask them, '*Can I help you?*'

In many cases there may be no apparent or easily identifiable way to offer your help, but maybe there's something under the surface. In these cases, you may need to explore and try to find ways you could help: treat it like a game. If you are in the company of another person, the simplest way you can begin to find out more is just to ask them, '*How are you?*' Then focus on them, repeat the questions, but keep them and their words directly in the forefront of your mind so you are actively in the moment. Try to find out more, dig, investigate. Talk. *Listen.* Somewhere in that conversation it's waiting for you, a moment, an opportunity that you can seize upon to help them. *Or maybe not.* Maybe there's nothing, no way you can help them at this time. But what will be remembered is that you asked the question, you listened to the response and the intention was there. The intention to help them.

HOW CAN I MAKE THEM SMILE?

The words within the questions are very specific, none more so than when we ask how we can make others smile. It sounds simple; surely everyone knows how to make someone else smile? Not so quick. 'Smile' is a simple word that can be interpreted in many different ways, and this can influence how successfully you implement this thought process. When we talked about how you can *help* others, we saw that the broad intent provides a universe of opportunity that you are free to readily explore, like the USS Enterprise skipping at warp speed from one planet to the next.

However, we need to be a little more cautious when asking how we can make someone smile; there is potential to over complicate and add confusion. It's important to understand the intent of the question: this is a simple question to help you *drive a positive engagement with another person.* A smile tells you that the person is reacting directly to something you may have said or done. That's all we're trying to achieve. *A smile.* No words, just a visual thumbs-up that they are reacting positively in whatever interaction you may have had. This could be:

- I am out running and let my thoughts wander through my family and friends. I consider my best friend, Simon, and some of the things that make us laugh. *I repeat the questions.* When I return home, I call him to catch up.
- I am in the kitchen with my wife preparing tea. We've both had a busy day. *I repeat the questions.* I ask about her day and keep my thoughts focussed on the discussion, continually looking for ways I can make her smile.
- I'm lying in bed, my mind busy with work. My thoughts drift to my mother and her upcoming birthday. *I repeat the questions.* I focus my thoughts on what we could do to make her day special.

There is a critical distinction here. I'm not trying to make them *happy*. Someone smiling is quite different to someone being happy. Happiness is an *internal* state of mind. A smile is different. It represents feedback on your engagement with another person and something you *can directly* influence.

You have limited control over other people's internal feelings and happiness. I spent years struggling with my mental health, and the question of whether I was happy or not was really something only I could resolve. Others played their part: kindness, friendship and love helped me, but my internal 'happy-o-meter' could only ever really be boosted by my own thoughts and actions. On the happiest and best of days, I could easily be in the saddest and worst of places.

If you set out to make another person *happy*, you are attempting to change their internal state of mind, and in some cases, this could be an impossible task. That's not to say it's a bad thing. I applaud Mr Happy for bumbling around Happyland like an oversized grapefruit and managing to bring Mr Miserable around to his way of thinking. That's no small achievement. We must remember what these questions are trying to do, though. This is all about providing *you* with a mechanism to reach out to others, for *you* to step away from the internal world and easily engage with the external world. You are not trying to save others; this is about saving *yourself.* The positive benefit others receive is just a side benefit.

Trying to make others *happy* can be futile, something that immediately pushes you away from stepping outside of your mind, something that keeps you locked in, thinking and plotting. It can also drive a sense of failure, especially if you start to relate the outcome of your actions to your own state of mind. Trying harder and harder to shift another person's way of thinking and seeing no change may make you think something isn't working. You try to make them happy. They remain sad. You see failure and reflect on what you are doing wrong. This is the absolute opposite of what we are trying to achieve. You might not be able to make them *happy*. But you can be in the moment rather than distant and distracted. You can think positive thoughts that may make them *smile*. You can ask questions that may lead to an opportunity for humour or conversation. Focus on what is possible: use this process to make *yourself* happy. The rest will fall into place. *Trust me.*

BRINGING THE QUESTIONS TOGETHER

Why does The Kind Mind Method work so well? Firstly, it provides you with a positive thought that can replace your negative ones. It's not just a positive mantra to try and give you confidence, this is about giving your brain something to directly engage with. These are not just words that you allow to wash over you, they are questions that *need* to be processed. More importantly, these questions are perfectly balanced to provide you with a route to the outside world. They are simple, broad and specific at the same time.

You can apply them to *any* situation or problem. You can use them when you are alone to mentally drift through people in your imagination or snap yourself into the moment by focussing on people in your physical presence. And the true magic? Even if you don't find an answer, you don't speak up or reach out, your thoughts will have all been positive. *Never forget this.* Simply repeating these words, asking these questions and putting your thoughts to good use, this is better than worry or fear. It will help you; it will free your thoughts, and then, ultimately, it will free you.

The balance of the questions is critical. This will always provide you with an alternative, a different option depending on the circumstances. If you take a one-dimensional approach to these questions, it pushes you into a corner, potentially forcing you into behaviour and situations that can cause further anxiety and stress. Helping others is a good thing, but if that were *everything*, it would soon become a burden. A responsibility that you could never live up to and that would only drive disappointment and a sense of failure. Make them smile? Imagine constantly aspiring to that;

there is no flexibility or nuance in this question alone. This thought process will drive some changes in your behaviour in both these situations. What matters is that you always have a different option to explore.

IN THE REAL WORLD: **ROAD RAGE**

"It was terrifying. He slammed his brakes on and came to a screeching halt. I just managed to stop. As I glanced up, he was already out of his car and striding towards me. I was shocked at the anger burning from his face and just had time to glance down and check my car door was locked.

It is hard to remember what he said. I do remember there was a lot of swearing, and I did notice his wife leap out of the passenger side of the car and join in at one point. I didn't say anything beyond a bewildered shrug of the shoulders.

After he returned to the car and drove off, and I had stopped shaking, my mind leapt into action. The possible responses I should have given. The righteous indignation I felt as the wronged party. The fear of ludicrous situations that might arise in the future. The thoughts burned within me, and I knew they had the potential to remain with me for days.

But they didn't. Each time the thought returned, I simply asked the questions. It wasn't easy at first, especially while I was driving on my own. But when I returned home to my family, it became easier as I focussed my positive thoughts on them. During the evening we went out with friends and once more I simply asked myself, 'How can I help them? How can I make them smile?' And then I looked out towards the friends surrounding me. The negative thoughts from the incident were still powerful and persistent, but with this process, it felt effortless to dismiss them.

It is hard to comprehend the difference the questions made. This was exactly the type of thought that I would typically fixate over for days. But with the help of these questions, it was nothing more than a belligerent shout from the sidelines of my mind. By the following day it was entirely gone."

SUMMARY

- When asking *how can I help them?* don't overthink the answer.
- You are not trying to make people happy. A simple *smile* tells you that you have had a positive engagement. That's enough.
- And remember, you always have an option: help *or* smile.

8

A KIND MIND

Some top tips.

OVERVIEW

To ensure *you* have the best opportunity of successfully embedding the thought process into your day-to-day thinking, this section provides some key tips across three key stages:

- **ADOPTING** a kind mind
- **USING** your kind mind
- **ENHANCING** your kind mind

ADOPTING A KIND MIND

1. THE FIRST FEW WEEKS

My use of these questions has reduced drastically since I first discovered them. These days it's like a fly swatter that I pull out to swipe away a nuisance thought: completely in my control and deployed with precision accuracy. This is very different from the first few weeks, where I would liken the use of it to a thermonuclear weapon of the mind: all-encompassing and destroying everything in its path. In those early days, my thinking was so immersed in negativity that only a drastic approach had any chance of working. Negative thoughts rained down, and I constantly repeated the questions.

From the moment I woke, I would crush the flutter of fear I felt by asking the questions. Relentlessly I would continue to ask the questions throughout the day. Hundreds, even thousands of times. My negative thoughts fought desperately to regain control, but I drowned them in positivity. And then, at the end of the day, lying in bed, with the gentle rumble of my wife snoring beside me, it would be the continual repetition of these questions that would guide me gently into sleep.

For this to work, you *must* embrace these questions wholeheartedly. You know your negative thoughts add no value whatsoever. You now have an option. A different thought. A *better* thought.

At first, it may sound strange. It may even *feel* strange. But it won't always be this way. Each and every time you engage with these outward-looking thoughts, you are stepping away from negative thinking. More importantly, you are constantly reinforcing this positive outlook.

Years after the weekend away in the Yorkshire Dales where I discovered these questions, I do still ask them every day. If I've had a challenging situation or thought, then there may be a flurry of activity to push me in the right direction. But most of the time, it's a gentle reminder once or twice a day that shifts my thinking in the right direction.

This is because I now approach my entire life with those two questions echoing gently within *every* thought and decision I make. I don't need to ask them directly because through the years of using this thought process, I've trained my brain to respond differently. This principal of choosing a better thought, of engaging with others and looking for ways I can help people or make them smile, has essentially become a part of my core personality. A guiding principle that has dropped to a deeper emotional level within me. Something I *just do* rather than actively have to make an effort with.

In every way, this has made my life immeasurably better. I see situations that will cause me stress and instinctively understand how to manage them. I can quickly identify negative thoughts and am able to effortlessly pivot away from them. And I continually search for ways to proactively engage with the people and world around me. All because I fully embraced these two simple questions.

"IN THE EARLY DAYS, IMMERSE YOURSELF IN THE THOUGHT PROCESS, REPEAT IT AGAIN AND AGAIN AND AGAIN."

2. CELEBRATE SUCCESS

It's important that you recognise and celebrate the positive change within you. Take some time, either in the moment or at the end of the day, to reflect upon your interaction with the wider world and consider the positive engagements you have had. This retrospection and analysis will help you take stock of the benefit the process provides and will continue to fuel your confidence to use the process on a day-to-day basis.

It may have been a simple hello to a stranger, or a question to a colleague, but if the outcome was driven from the questions, it is a tangible shift from your previous state of mind. You must remember that this action, however small and inconsequential, simply would not have existed before. The questions have driven a tangible and real change, created a positive moment that you have shared with another person.

"STOP AND REFLECT ON THE POSITIVE ACTIONS THIS THOUGHT PROCESS HAS CREATED."

3. AND DON'T FORGET THE VERY IMPORTANT POINT...

The thought process should never place a burden on you to help anyone or make them smile. The words are intended as an inquisitive thought that allows you to shift *your* internal thinking. It is constructed in a perfect way to allow you multi-dimensional engagement with other people that can drive an inspiring change. The key element is that you are changing *your* way of thinking. There are no external obligations. The change is within you.

There is an additional aspect to consider in this regard. At the beginning of this book, I asked you to limit the number of people you speak to about the process as you adopt it. There's a simple reason for this. Almost universally when I talk to people about this thought process, they focus on the outcome. The good deeds. The positive actions that are being undertaken. As we know, these are indeed important and are a key part of the ongoing success of this process, but they are not the ultimate objective you are seeking.

If others misunderstand the purpose and focus on this outcome, they may bring with them unrealistic expectations. *Shouldn't you be making me smile? Shouldn't you be helping me?* Even innocent comments or offhand jokes along these lines can impact the effectiveness of the questions. For this to work, there should be no pressure upon yourself. Helping others and making them smile are not obligations to be met. When others question this, in whatever context, it raises doubt. Worry. Negative thoughts. You start shifting your measure of success to an external, and often unachievable, outcome. *This change is all within you.*

Yes, these questions will *push* you outward, encourage you to speak out where before you may have remained quiet. And I urge you to take on the challenge and act upon these questions whenever you can; this remains a critical factor in the success of this process. But remember, the purpose of The Kind Mind Method is to help *you* manage negative thoughts. Everything else, the positive actions, the kindness displayed to others, is simply a bonus. The free gift you found in the bottom of your cereal box as a child. So, repeat the words, challenge yourself and reach out to the wider world at every opportunity, but feel no regret at the times you don't speak out. Simply rejoice in the positive thoughts you are having.

"THE KIND MIND METHOD IS INTENDED TO HELP YOU. EVERYTHING ELSE IS JUST A BONUS."

USING YOUR KIND MIND

1. KEEP IT SIMPLE

When you are actively engaging with other people through this thought process, regardless of whether they are strangers or acquaintances, there will often be no simple answer to the questions. You may not immediately see any way to help them or make them smile. This is fine. While you ask the questions, you are constantly considering positive ways to engage.

The simplest approach in these situations is to start a conversation. It may not give you an immediate answer, it may not illicit a smile or help anyone, but it can be the first step on the path towards that outcome. A simple 'How are you?' may be enough, or even better, 'Can I help you?' Who knows where it will lead? Even if the conversation goes nowhere, it is *something*. You created that moment from the use of this process, and it would not have existed otherwise.

When you are asking the questions in the presence of other people, there is an additional tip that I recommend. *Make a deal with yourself.* A mental handshake that whenever you start repeating the questions, you will not stop until you have started a conversation or carried out some positive act. You may find you repeat them once and something quickly comes to mind. Or it could be ten, twenty or more repetitions. But it *will* happen. You *will* reach out. And the entire time before will be filled with positive thoughts about how you can engage with others rather than anxiety about what you might say or what they may be thinking.

This tip can be used repeatedly, and you will be continually rewarded for your effort. The conversations you have started. The subsequent places they may take you to. All because you committed to engaging positively with the people around you.

"START WITH A SIMPLE CONVERSATION WHEN ENGAGING WITH OTHERS."

2. GREAT IDEA

The success of this process is absolutely built around the dual ability to stop you from thinking negative thoughts *and* help you to consider positive ways to interact with the wider world. As you repeat the two simple questions, your initial state of mind may see them as a hazy concept that is just there to stop you from worrying, but as the words are repeated and your mind begins to consider the question, you will engage and analyse. Your aim is to consider your surroundings, your circle of friends (old and new), your family, your work colleagues, or, quite simply, people within your vicinity, and try to mentally answer one of the questions.

Quite often there's no obvious answer. But that doesn't mean you should give up. You can remain focussed on the same focal point, and each time you deploy the process, consider different options or ways to engage. Persevering and thinking creatively about how you engage will always help deliver better results and wider engagement. If you can't think of any way to engage? Simply shift your focus onto someone different and start the thought process again.

But what if your mind wanders and drifts away from the core set of questions you were repeating? This creative use of the questions will often act as a catalyst for daydreams, and the curiosity of the mind may lead you in many different directions. As long as these thoughts remain positive, then feel free to indulge and embrace your thinking. I remain as immersed in my daydreams now as the time when I was depressed. The only difference is that all my thoughts are now positive.

"THINK CREATIVELY AND EMBRACE POSITIVE DAYDREAMS."

3. TRUST THE PROCESS

When you are asking these questions in the reactive context to manage a *negative* thought, it can take time for the initial thought to stop echoing through your mind. Mentally, it sticks like chewing gum to the carpet and can become almost impossible to remove. In these instances, you must *trust the process* and keep asking the questions.

It doesn't matter if you action them, or who the intended recipient is; the intent is to try and see the thought process through until such point the negative thoughts fade into the background. Repeat the words, but most importantly, flick through that mental list of friends, family and colleagues, or search the people around you and try to think of some small way you could help them or make them smile. If you can't think of anything, *keep trying*. Commit to finding at least one answer for one person. Where possible, try and bring your good intentions to life by making it happen.

If the negative thought still remains, *simply start again*. At times, it will be difficult. But every single repetition of these questions will take you further away from the original thought and ultimately allow your mind to drift onto something different and more positive.

> **"HOWEVER POWERFUL YOUR NEGATIVE THOUGHTS ARE, TRUST THE PROCESS AND KEEP ASKING THE QUESTIONS."**

ENHANCING YOUR KIND MIND

1. SORT IT

It is only now, as I look back at the worries that drove my anxiety and negative thinking, that I can truly see how inconsequential most of them were. I worried about what I had said, done or written. I worried about what *might* happen. In all cases, my worry had no tangible benefit or output beyond damaging my mental and physical health. None. Whatsoever. Not that I would necessarily have accepted that at the time.

This isn't to say there may not be some action or output that could change *some* of the situations. This is where I believe you can give yourself the space and perspective to look at a worry in a different way. When you ask the questions and your mind shifts away from negative thoughts, you can view your initial worry with perspective. And the critical question to consider is whether you have done everything you can to address the situation. If you are worrying about your health, do you have a doctor's appointment? If you are worrying about work, is there anything you can change? If you are worrying about family, what action can you take?

The questions free you from the immediate worry and provide you with the mental space to think creatively about the issue at hand. In many cases you may be able to focus the questions onto the person who is the source of your worry and it will give you an alternative approach to looking at the problem.

In some cases, though, there will be times when there is nothing you can do. Some problems cannot be fixed, and your fear may well be real. I am aware there could be a day when my hypochondria finally becomes a reality. And if, or when, that day does come, I will still have this same choice. I can fear the inevitable, turn inward and isolate myself from others in the limited time I have left by worrying about a future I cannot change. Or I can embrace the people around me and consider how I can make our time together more memorable. I can ask myself: ***How can I help them? How can I make them smile?***

"WHERE YOU CAN, ADDRESS THE UNDERLYING ISSUE."

2. DIFFERENT PERSPECTIVE

Depression fuels fear. It is for this reason that almost every decision, issue or problem I faced through my years of negative thinking became a *worry.* Even the simplest of challenges could be an insurmountable catastrophe for my worry-filled mind. These questions can help you strip away the worry and reveal the *decision* within.

Take, for example, my wife's fortieth birthday. I was becoming anxious about the impending celebrations. Several of her friends had recently hit the same milestone, and the ever-expanding range of surprise parties, weekends away and extravagant gifts was building the mental pressure within me. No gift felt right, and no party felt special enough. My anxiety grew as each subsequent celebration closed the door on another idea and mounted more pressure on me. It affected my ability to think rationally. And then, the ultimate question, *What should I get my wife for her fortieth birthday?* was reframed into a worry: *I can't get my wife anything for her birthday as it will never be good enough.* In reality, this was all in my head. A delayed decision that grew into a worry.

Asking the two questions enabled me to stop fixating on the frustration I felt at not being able to find the right gift. Each repetition allowed me to step away from the situation I had created. My thoughts became free and I was no longer annoyed at my wife for having the temerity to be turning forty and having friends who had done so several months earlier.

I was still left with a decision, though. Not just a decision, but one that the questions could help me with. ***How can I help them? How can I make them smile?*** I asked the questions and mentally focussed on my wife and started thinking about potential gifts. Instead of fearing the situation, I faced directly into it from a *different perspective.* The worry simply vanished as I repeated the questions and focussed entirely on my wife. How I could help her. How I could make her smile.

"USE THE PROCESS TO TURN A WORRY INTO A SIMPLE DECISION OR ACTION."

3. HELP YOURSELF

I have always had a creative mind, and writing has been a continual source of mental wellbeing and inspiration to me. The act of imagining, creating and inspiring with my work replenishes my energy for life. It gives me a purpose beyond my family and my job. Something specifically for me, and me alone. Through the years when I was depressed, I was fearful of letting my mind wander and unable to write. I felt the loss like a physical ailment, and this fuelled further negative thinking.

Since I started using this thought process, the enjoyment has been back. I can let my mind wander; no longer do I fear where it will take me. Most importantly, I have *something*. A thing I can do and enjoy. Something to enrich my life, something positive.

Statistically speaking, it is unlikely you are a writer, but I do believe it is important that you have something to focus your body and mind. Something just for you, something that you enjoy, a treat for your emotional self. Running, reading, writing, painting. Join a club or find a hobby. It really doesn't matter what it is. The important thing is that you are using some of that spare brain capacity on an activity *you* enjoy. That gives, rather than steals, your energy.

The Kind Mind Method can give you back the space to explore and create. It's up to you to decide what you do with that freedom of thought.

"LOOK TO FIND PHYSICAL OR MENTAL ACTIVITIES THAT CAN SUPPORT YOUR WELLBEING."

SUMMARY

ADOPTING A KIND MIND:

1. In the early days, immerse your thoughts in the thought process, repeat it again and again and again.
2. Stop and reflect on the positive actions this thought process has created.
3. The Kind Mind Method is intended to help *you*. Everything else is just a bonus.

USING YOUR KIND MIND:

1. Start with a simple conversation when engaging with others.
2. Think creatively and embrace positive daydreams.
3. However powerful your negative thoughts are, *trust the process,* and keep asking the questions.

ENHANCING YOUR KIND MIND:

1. Where you can, address the underlying issue.
2. Use the process to turn a worry into a simple decision or action.
3. Look to find physical or mental activities that can support your wellbeing.

EPILOGUE

Handing it over.

HOW CAN I HELP THEM? HOW CAN I MAKE THEM SMILE?

This cognitive tool allows me to step away from negative thoughts. It pushes me to engage with the wider world. It gives my mind space to think freely and it gently guides me towards having a better outlook on life. It does all of this because I am not complacent. I don't take this positive mindset for granted; I continue to repeat these special words every single day. My triggers have reduced drastically, but they are still there. I remain vigilant. I continue to use this thought process. I have embraced a *Kind Mind.*

So, with these final words, it is the end of our journey together and, hopefully, the start of a new one for you. At the beginning of this book, I asked you not to use this thought process until you had finished the book. My belief is that you need all the information, the context, the tips and tricks, to really ensure it works. *But now is the time.* There is no more reading to be done.

These first few days may seem strange. You may feel uncertain about the constant repetition. But I urge you to immerse yourself as you begin to ask these questions.

Shift all your negative thoughts by constantly repeating these familiar words. Pre-empt additional negative thoughts by asking them in the proactive context. Focus on friends, family and colleagues to increase your engagement and move your thinking to a more outward-looking mode. Browse the sea of strangers around you and consider how you can interact with them. Use them in social situations to snap you into the present moment.

How can I help them?
How can I make them smile?

For a long time after the transformative weekend away, I referred to these questions as *my* thought process. As if I had some direct influence or role in their creation. But I see things very differently now. This was a *discovery*. A revelation that came to me through time and circumstance. A magical truth that existed for *anyone* to reach out and grasp. And from that day forward, my role in all of this has been simple: to share my discovery.

So here, Dear Reader, is the final moment of change. This process is *yours* now, all of it. To help you. To change you. To enable you to become the person you aspire to be.

I hope, truly, that one day this means as much to you as it does to me.

The end.

ACKNOWLEDGEMENTS

I read a lot. And almost always, when I get to the end of a book, I spend a brief few moments reading the acknowledgements. Maybe that is because I am an aspiring author myself and am subconsciously searching for some insight that will help my own creative output. Or maybe there is simply a desire to hold onto a friendly and familiar voice for a few moments longer. Or maybe it is pure curiosity.

I don't know what my own reasons are, which means I have even less of an idea about your motivation. But if you are still with me, maybe reading onwards with little or no understanding of why, I would like to offer a brief reward for your perseverance. Thank *you.* Thank you for staying with me. For reading this book. For sharing part of my journey. If my story has resonated with you, if you are able to take these questions forward and embrace them in any small way, then you should know that this book was written entirely with *you* in mind.

Publishing a book for the first time has been a very challenging experience and this book would not exist in its current form without the help, support, creative input and guidance of many people.

I would like to start with my most ardent supporters: Mum and Dad. It is not only your relentless interest and encouragement that I am thankful for. There are three key ingredients that have brought this book to life: positivity, creativity and effort. And within each of these traits that I have relied upon, I understand *exactly* where they came from. I see them within both of *you*. Dad, your positive outlook on all aspects of life. Mum, your thoughtfulness, insight and empathy. And jointly, the work ethic that you instilled within me. Never telling me to work harder. Simply doing it yourselves and setting an example that has propelled me through my adult life. I may not say it often enough, but I love you both. Thank you for *everything*.

To Jodie, Jake and Richard – thank you for you love and support.

To *'Coach Caroline.'* Your support and coaching throughout the past year has been a great help to me. Allowing me to talk through my thoughts, structuring my tasks, being a sounding board for ideas and providing feedback to my presentations. For all of this and much more, thank you. This was my first foray into coaching and I am extremely glad that I was able to find you. Shameless plug alert: https://coachyourlife.co.uk

To Simon Nixon. I could thank you for your continual encouragement, candour and feedback whilst writing this book – all of which was greatly appreciated and has influenced the end result more than you probably know. But more importantly, thank you for *always* being there for me.

To Matt Telfer. We have never met, but it is not hyperbole to say that your editorial input saved this book. I was blinded in two critical areas and without your guidance, I believe the end result would have been compromised and confusing. Your feedback gave me clarity; it helped me truly believe in myself and the power of this thought process. Thank you.

To Soufyane Zanfoukh. Thank you for bringing my ideas to life with your drawings. And for being so patient as I continually changed my mind throughout the design stages.

To *everyone* who volunteered and distributed one of my envelopes. Your kindness is my inspiration.

To Sarah Lahay. Thank you for your design expertise and guidance.

To Paddy Hartnett. Seriously. Above and beyond. When I read your email it was a pivotal point in this whole journey. A moment where my thought process stepped beyond the confines of my own mind and extended to others. *Your* kindness. Your offer of support. For no other reason than to *help me*. To make *me smile*. Your generosity moved me deeply. Thank you. I removed this section from the document you proofread so any grammatical errors are entirely on me.

To Jake Humphrey and Damian Hughes. Probably the people who are least likely to read this, but like everything I do, I have hope. I started listening to your podcast on a recommendation from my wife. I was sceptical at first. It didn't quite sound my thing. But I could not have been more wrong. *The High Performance* podcast has been my constant companion and inspiration throughout the entire time I have been writing this book. As I struggled to balance my work, family and writing, I would listen to you interviewing a guest about the importance of purpose and it would remind me of why I was doing this. When I suffered a setback, an episode would miraculously appear to educate me about resilience and how I can learn from my failures. One of your guests (Mo Gawdat) profoundly shaped the direction of this book. He inspired me and provided an understanding that required the difficult (but essential) step to scrap an entire second draft. Your weekly words have been a true journey of growth for me. Thank you both.

I have saved the most important thank you to the end. My family. Clare, my wife. And my two children, Dexter and Brodie. Neither of my children know much of this story and their pivotal role within it. Their interest extends only to '*Daddy is writing a book*' and '*can we buy it on Amazon?*' But they remain my proudest joy in life. And, finally, to Clare. There was a brief moment where I toyed with the idea of calling this book '*be more like Clare.*' The concept of helping others and making them smile is built into your DNA – it requires no prompt – you just do it. You are the positive Ying to my worrisome Yang. I know I do not say it enough, but thank you. I appreciate everything you do and everything you are. I love you. This book is dedicated to *you.* Always. X

NOTES

This book has been a hugely personal journey, and my objective throughout has always been clear: pass this thought process on in the simplest way possible. For this reason, it was always intended to be based on my own experience rather than a commentary on the broader approaches to addressing negative thinking and depression.

As I progressed through the years, and the multiple drafts, it became clear that much of what I had discovered did indeed align with a significant amount of scientific thinking in certain areas, especially kindness to others. I was fortunate that a lot of information had already been gathered and presented in a much more accessible way than I could ever possibly hope to achieve. Detailed below are the key reference points I used within my brief foray into the world of kindness and interrogative self-talk.

1. Senay, I., Albarracín, D., & Noguchi, K. (2010). Motivating goal-directed behaviour through introspective self-talk: the role of the interrogative form of simple future tense. *Psychological Science, 21*(4), 499–504.

2. The Kindness Test https://www.sussex.ac.uk/research/centres/kindness/research/thekindnesstest

3. Claudia Hammond's excellent book *The Keys to Kindness* is the best place to start if you have any questions about kindness. Using the data from the kindness study and cross-referencing wider research, it provides the definitive guide on the power of kindness to help both yourself and others.

4. Rowland, L., & Curry, O. S. (2019). A range of kindness activities boost happiness. *The Journal of social psychology, 159*(3), 340–343. https://doi.org/10.1080/00224545.2018.1469461

Printed in Great Britain
by Amazon

29496354R00117